Praise for

OWNER OF A LONELY HEART

"As Nguyen puts these experiences into writing, a healing recognition occurs, most movingly through her children, who are able to see and validate things she cannot."

—*The Washington Post*

"A portrait of things left unsaid . . . Nguyen seems aware that her anxieties are small in comparison to the existential sacrifice her family made. But this is a memoir for those late-night moments: deeply ruminative."

—*The New York Times Book Review*

"In this achingly beautiful look at her relationship with her mother, Nguyen unpacks the toll of the Vietnam War, when, due to the chaos, her family was split apart. She, her father, and her sister eventually land in Grand Rapids, and her mother, in Boston, Nguyen only rediscovering her whereabouts at age 10. Just how the legacy of their loss divides them is told with wrenching emotion and exquisite controlled prose. A soon-to-be classic with implications about immigration in any era."

—*Oprah Daily*

"Affecting . . . The book is filled with honest and sometimes painful insights that Nguyen discovers in her search for truths about the past."

—*New York Journal of Books*

"The author—whose father fled with her from Saigon in 1975—considers her fraught, scant relationship with her biological mother, other formative maternal connections, and her own role as a mom to her sons in this thoughtful excavation."

—*Vanity Fair*

"*Owner of a Lonely Heart* is not a chronological memoir. It circulates among memories, embellishing and deepening the reader's and Nguyen's understanding of them. . . . A superb writer, Nguyen gives readers a tactile sense of her childhood home life and the love and anguish she felt there."

—*BookPage*

"Nguyen grapples with vital questions of family, loss, and memory, giving voice to the oft overlooked contours of grief—and encouraging readers to reflect on their own relationships."

—*The Christian Science Monitor*

"Nguyen is a confident and reliable protagonist even when running up against painful memories, providing readers with enough distance as to almost be objective. . . . Nguyen has made a journey of facing her origins and contending with the limitations of American narratives, and we are lucky to be invited along the way."

—*The Brooklyn Rail*

"Quietly moving . . . A ruminative, unadorned, lyrical look at origins, family, and belonging."

—*Kirkus Reviews*

"Shines as a multilayered look at the ways absence can shape one's sense of self."

—*Publishers Weekly*

"Poignant . . . Beautifully written and painfully honest, Nguyen's memoir reveals the struggles and prejudices refugees face and the importance of knowing your life story."

—*Booklist*

"Beth Nguyen has created a new way to ache that is as comfortable exploring loss, loneliness, and longing as it is exploring the contours of joy, survival, and, really, the kind of fleshy isolation necessary to make lasting art. The premise here is so compelling, but the execution is otherworldly. Every page of *Owner of a Lonely Heart* will have you holding your chest with one hand while eagerly turning the page with the other. This book, and the making of lives it explores, is what memoir writing in the hands of a caring, curious wunderkind can be."

—Kiese Laymon, author of
Heavy: An American Memoir

"*Owner of a Lonely Heart* is the autobiography of a feeling—the story of a fear you cannot name because you are one of the authors, a secret you hid even from yourself in case even this might save you. Nguyen unravels the way the child refugee she was learned to save herself, which turns out to be the final act of saving oneself—not from the country she left, but the country she found. This memoir is a distillation, the sort of cure you make from a poison but can offer to others, and she has written it with a direct, spotlit brilliance, page by careful page."

—Alexander Chee, author of
How to Write an Autobiographical Novel

"Nguyen's triumph of a book is forged and fed by her searing curiosity about her refugee family's past and her jeweler's eye for precise detail—all while navigating the geography of her Midwest roots with a big, beautiful heart. A must-read for all who struggle with or celebrate complicated family. This will nourish, rend, and tend your heart."

—Aimee Nezhukumatathil,
author of *World of Wonders*

"*Owner of a Lonely Heart* is, quite possibly, the most beautiful memoir I've ever read. It is a book about history, about family, about where and to whom we belong, and whether we ever really do. Devastating in both its sharpness and its compassion, this book is a masterpiece—truly, a gift."

—Lacy M. Johnson,
author of *The Reckonings*

"This brilliant, searching memoir clinches Beth Nguyen's place among the great writers and thinkers of our day."

—Joanna Rakoff, author of
My Salinger Year and *A Fortunate Age*

ALSO BY BETH NGUYEN

Stealing Buddha's Dinner: A Memoir

Short Girls: A Novel

Pioneer Girl: A Novel

OWNER OF A LONELY HEART

A Memoir of Motherhood and Absence

Beth Nguyen

SCRIBNER

New York   London   Toronto   Sydney   New Delhi

Scribner
An Imprint of Simon & Schuster, LLC
1230 Avenue of the Americas
New York, NY 10020

First Scribner trade paperback edition May 2024

SCRIBNER and design are trademarks of Simon & Schuster, LLC

Simon & Schuster: Celebrating 100 Years of Publishing in 2024

For information about special discounts for bulk purchases,
please contact Simon & Schuster Special Sales at 1-866-506-1949
or business@simonandschuster.com.

The Simon & Schuster Speakers Bureau can bring authors to your live event. For more information, or to book an event, contact the Simon & Schuster Speakers Bureau at 1-866-248-3049 or visit our website at www.simonspeakers.com.

Interior design by Davina Mock-Maniscalco

Manufactured in the United States of America

10   9   8   7   6   5   4   3   2   1

Library of Congress Cataloging-in-Publication Data has been applied for.

ISBN 978-1-9821-9634-9
ISBN 978-1-9821-9635-6 (pbk)
ISBN 978-1-9821-9636-3 (ebook)

CONTENTS

1. Twenty-Four Hours   1

2. Apparent, Part I   11

3. Date of Birth   43

4. The Photograph   61

5. Apparent, Part II   89

6. Apparent, Part III   113

7. My Mothers   131

8. White Mothers   157

9. The Story of My Name   183

10. Apparent, Revisited   199

    Acknowledgments   235

1

TWENTY-FOUR HOURS

Over the course of my life I have known less than twenty-four hours with my mother. Here is how those hours came to be, and what happened in them.

I grew up in Michigan, in a mostly white town in the 1980s, pretending not to be a refugee. Back then, the idea was to forget the past and move along. Stay out of trouble. Don't talk about the war. Don't react to racist taunts. Behave well enough not to get noticed. And that's what I did. I did my homework and watched television and climbed the neighbor's plum tree. But every spring I would think about how my family had left Saigon the day before the fall of the city and the end of the war—what is known in Vietnam as the American War. I was a baby, carried by my dad and uncles and grandmother, brought by motorcycle, boat, ship, and airplane to refugee camps and eventually to a home in the United States. I would try to imagine this: literally fleeing a country, not knowing what would happen next.

It was my grandmother Noi who made the final call. She had done it before, leaving her birthplace of Hanoi for the south, when the country was divided in 1954. By the time we arrived in the United States, in the summer of 1975, she was fifty-five years old, a refugee twice over. I asked her once, years ago, How did you decide? She said, You just know. You just go. At the time, I thought it was an unsatisfying answer. That's how far I was from understanding what she must have gone through.

When we left, my mother stayed in Saigon, or was left behind in Saigon. For many years, I wouldn't know which phrasing was more true. But I knew not to ask about it, because no one in my family wanted to talk about my mother and no one wanted to talk about the war. I grew up knowing these were silences that needed to be kept. And it wasn't even hard, because I had no actual memories of war and leaving. I had the privilege, instead, of getting to imagine. Silence can look like submission, but for many of us it can be a form of self-preservation.

I was ten years old when I learned that my mother had come to the United States as a refugee, too. I was nineteen when I finally met her.

The known hours I have spent with my mother have been bounded by years and miles of absence. They have taken place over six visits and twenty-six years. Always in Boston, the city where she eventually landed. Toward the end of a visit she will look at me, sitting next to her on a sofa or at a table in her apartment, and she will give a small, tired smile as if to convey, What else is there? What else is there to say? I have never called her Mom. Our hours together have been defined by what we do not say. By now, silence is the language we have with each other, and the one we know best.

The person I call Mom is my stepmom, whom my dad met and married when I was three. In real life, when I talk about *my mom* I'm talking about her. I use the word *step-mom* here, in my writing, only because the limits of language require such distinctions.

What I'm saying is that I grew up with a mom and a grandmother and I was lucky to have so much. I had no right to ask for more.

———

Refugees don't fit the romantic immigrant narrative that's so dominant in America. They are a more obvious, uncomfortable reminder of war and loss. And too often, as scholar Yến Lê Espiritu points out, the "history of US military, economic, and political intervention . . . is often included only as background information—as the events that *precede* the refugee flight rather than as the actions that *produce* this very exodus." Part of my own refugee condition is realizing that I have participated in this kind of rhetoric and erasure.

America can be ruthless to newcomers. Refugees—those who are even allowed in this country at all—are expected to become relatively self-sufficient within a year. They are supposed to pay back the cost of travel to get to the United States. And they are expected to be absolutely grateful. I watched my dad and uncles and grandmother struggle— sometimes with English, sometimes with the strange habits of Americans. Always there was a sense of not knowing how things were supposed to be done. Who would even think to tell us? In your first experience of winter and snow, how would you know what to do with an iced-over windshield? In a pre-internet world, how would you know there was a thing called a scraper? What if you threw boiling water on the car, thinking this would surely melt the ice, having no idea the glass would explode? What if in trying to navigate this new cold world you tried to ask questions at stores, but people just stared and said, I can't understand you. Speak up. Speak English. What if people told you to go back to where you came from, all the time, as if you could, and looked at you as the enemy because they didn't really understand the war and to them all Vietnamese were the same?

———

Growing up, I was afraid all the time. It was a low-lying fear that I couldn't explain to myself or dare admit out loud. It kept me awake at night, made me feel both too seen and unseen. I think now that I was afraid of all that my family still had to figure out about American life—how far from being settled or self-sufficient we actually were. It's why I learned to read early and copied inflected dialogue from TV shows. I memorized words, perfected them. I won school spelling bees. I tried to live in libraries. In school, I watched and learned whatever my white friends did. What they wore. What they brought for lunch. Their idioms and slang. I could be almost just like them, so long as I avoided the mirror and used powerful forms of denial whenever I was at home. I thought I could transcend my origins, as if I were never a refugee, as if I were American born, as I sometimes pretended to be. As if that would protect me.

My dad has a photograph of himself in Saigon, leaning against his prized Yamaha motorcycle. He is so young—he was twenty-eight when we left Vietnam—his hair full and wavy. His smile is a gambler's smile. Later that motorcycle would get us from our house to the Saigon River, where we would find passage on a boat that would make its way to a U.S. naval ship out on the sea. My dad abandoned the motorcycle, of course, leaving it on the riverbank with the key because someone else would need it. His first ten years in America, he worked at a feather factory. He tried to keep the down out of his black hair, but it would settle on his jacket and clothes, a fine casting of dust that smelled to me like old sleep and Sunday mornings.

Fall is the word people always use when describing April 30, 1975, the day North Vietnamese forces took over Saigon, famously crashing tanks through the gates of the presidential palace. Whenever I heard that word, *fall*, I imagined bodies and buildings in slow-motion collapse. I still imagine it, because I cannot really know it. Not that day, nor the day before it—the chaos and flight, families trying to leave because there seemed no other choice.

Gallup polls from 1975 show that most Americans were against the idea of Vietnamese resettlement in the United States; polls from today show similar feelings toward refugees and asylum seekers from non-European countries. I wouldn't have needed a poll, back when I was growing up, to know that that was true. And maybe this is why the word *refugee* felt suffused with shame. As artist and scholar Trinh T. Minh-ha has said, "For general Western spectatorship, Vietnam does not exist outside of the war." The only narratives I heard about the war came from white people and their movies. Their gaze, their versions, their depiction of Vietnamese bodies as disposable, sites of violence and blame, determined the story that most Americans knew.

The prevailing message to refugees and immigrants is a demand for value: prove that you belong here; prove that you have any right to exist here. Show how much work you can do. The good refugee is invariably described as gracious, which is to say grateful. You can't just be a person. And if you're Asian in America, you'll always be regarded as foreign, at least a little bit suspect, a possible carrier of diseases and viruses. For those of us who grew up here, it's nearly impossible to avoid the effect of these views.

"When does a refugee stop being a refugee?" In asking this question, scholar Vinh Nguyen pursues the idea of "refugeetude," an identity that "is not temporally constrained to singular events (displacement, asylum seeking, resettlement), spatially tied to specific locations (the boat, the border, the camp), or bound to the letter of the law. Instead, it is psychic, affective, and embodied."

My relationship with the word *refugee* has paralleled my relationship with the word *mother*. Both weighty constructs, infused with assumptions. For much of my life, I felt uncomfortable with both words, a deep sense of shame. Because how could I even say them when I didn't really know what they meant?

One morning, not long after my second child was born, I got up from a night of broken sleep with a sentence in my mind. I wrote it down: *When I became a mother, I became a refugee.* It took a long time to make sense of it: how inhabiting motherhood has made me inhabit the refugee identity that I hadn't thought belonged to me, or hadn't wanted to belong to me. But I cannot be a mother without thinking about my mothers, cannot raise children without thinking about how I was raised. In every instance, in the back of my mind, I am here, I am a mother, because I was once, because I am still, a refugee. Meaning, all the political and cultural forces that have shaped me are still shaping me. Meaning, I am always carrying my family's stories with me, even the ones I don't know, the ones I don't know how to ask about. Every refugee has to bear the story of leaving. In my case, my dad and uncles fought in the war and lost. They weren't special or rich or high-ranking; we got out because we were lucky. We didn't know where we would end up. I lost a mother and a country and, eventually, a language. Now I'm a mother, with children who were born in the United States, children who know the word *refugee* more as concept than identity.

I am in between: the one and a half generation of people who were born in one country but raised in another.

A once-refugee and child of refugees. An uncertain-space, liminal state, partial refugee, where all the gaps are filled with shame. I am in between mothers, in between parents, in between loss, trying to understand how the past keeps changing because we keep changing. I am hiding in plain sight. An American citizen not by birth but by need. I took the tests and paid the fees. And every April, like so many Vietnamese, I think about 1975. I try to imagine. The exit, the unknown, the trust in chance. I look at that photo of my dad with his motorcycle and am astonished by how far it has traveled, intact, across so much water and land. It is an artifact, one of the only family heirlooms we have. It is a reminder, too, of how much was left and lost. Like our bodies and our faces, it is proof of our history and of how we got here.

2

APPARENT, PART 1

When my first child turned a year old, I brought him to Boston to meet my mother. She didn't show up. Later I learned that she had gone to Foxwoods Casino instead, which sounds bad and maybe was, but it had been a few years since I'd seen or even spoken to her; we wouldn't see each other again for seven more. I couldn't blame her for wanting to try her luck elsewhere.

"Birth mother" isn't the right phrase for her and neither is "biological mother," which implies an adoption story. I never know how to refer to the woman who gave birth to me, who was my first mother, who did not leave me but who was left by me. Sometimes I simply say "Boston mother," deflecting the adjective onto geography even though she ended up there not by choice, exactly, but by resettlement efforts years after the end of the war in Vietnam.

There's a long story here and it's one I keep having to tell, trying to understand it. Because there is no getting away from our origin stories.

When I have to explain to people how my family got to the United States, what I usually say is that we left Saigon the day before its fall. What I don't always say is that *family* meant my dad, uncles, grandmother, sister, and me, and that we left because my dad and uncles had been in the South Vietnamese military and the end of the war meant reeducation camps, or worse. What I say is that we made it to a boat on a river that went out to the sea where a U.S. naval ship picked us up and brought us to a refugee camp in the Philippines. From there, another camp in Guam and a third camp at Fort Chaffee in Arkansas, and then a new home in Grand Rapids, Michigan, because the federal government wanted refugees to be relocated across the country. What I leave out is that, technically, the first place we landed in the United States was Alaska, where the jet that was transporting our group of refugees stopped to refuel. I don't mention that when we got to Michigan we spent our first nights in a Holiday Inn, paid for by a church sponsor while he found us a place to live.

I almost never mention my mother—what happened

to her, and how I don't even know the story, exactly. It was wartime. Half of my family became refugees and half did not. Until I was ten years old, all my sister and I knew about our mother was that she had stayed in Vietnam. Every once in a rare while, if my dad was in a buoyant mood, drinking but not yet drunk, he might reminisce about his childhood. A rooster they had, their cat who had a pet rat, places they went fishing, games they played. He might even talk about getting out of Saigon the night of April 29. How he had left his motorcycle at the river; how he had befriended the captain of the naval ship in order to get milk and extra rice for me and my sister. These were meant to be thrilling stories and they were, tinged with the sense of the faraway.

Back then, my dad was not a person who smiled easily, or who allowed defiance. We had ended up in a mostly white community that wasn't happy about the arrival of a couple of hundred Vietnamese refugees, even though resettlement had been initiated by Gerald Ford, who had grown up in Grand Rapids. The tension of belonging or not belonging, of being stared at and overlooked, would come to define my entire childhood and adolescence.

If you had asked ten-year-old me to describe my family, I would have said that I lived with two sisters, a brother, two uncles, my grandmother, and my parents. We lived in a house on Florence Street and had a dog who liked to hide our shoes.

I would not have told you what that really meant, which was that I had a sister who was a year older; a stepsister who was my stepmom's daughter and who was several years older than I; a half brother who was born to my dad and stepmom when I was four; two uncles who were my dad's brothers; a third uncle who was actually a good family friend; a paternal grandmother, Noi; a dad; and a stepmom. Do you see the complications here, the openings for questions? It was better not to say too much. Better not to leave a space for people to ask, What about your mother?

A multigenerational, extended-family household is not unusual in much of the rest of the world, but it was, and maybe still is, in much of midwestern or suburban America. None of my friends in elementary school had families like mine; no one else even had a stepmom. That's probably why the TV shows I gravitated to were ones that featured non-traditional arrangements, like *The Facts of Life* and *Diff'rent Strokes*, where mother figures stand in for those who were absent, dead, or out of the picture. These were comedies, where everything in the world of the screen was made all right by the end of the half hour. But sometimes I would think about how much rested on the unspoken—who *wasn't* there that made the *there* people possible.

At home on Florence Street, my grandmother Noi did almost all the cooking and much of the cleaning. She knitted and gardened and looked after us kids, and she was almost always at home. My uncles were often home, too, depending on their work shifts, and they gave us lots of ice cream and lots of music—Simon & Garfunkel, the Eagles, Santana. My stepmom asked about homework; told us we were watching too much television; made us mind our bedtimes; went on errands; scolded us to clean our rooms; asked if we brushed our teeth; called out, Good night, sugar—but mostly she went to work, administrative jobs in secondary and community education, and there were days she would come home so tired that she'd ask one of us kids to help her take off her boots. My dad was working, too, at the feather factory, but mostly he was busy making friends with other Vietnamese refugees who'd been settled in the area. As the community continued to grow, centered around weekend poker parties and a new store called Saigon Market, that's where he wanted to be.

I wish I could pinpoint how I learned to be okay with the mystery of having another mother in another country, a place that so mystified me that whenever I looked at a globe or world map I would find Vietnam and Saigon— now listed as Ho Chi Minh City—and not quite believe that I had been born there. Once, when my sister Anh and I were little enough to take baths together and share a twin bed, her whispered voice in the darkness—Do you think our mother is alive?—made me realize I had already wondered the same. We almost never talked about this, though, because what was there to say? No one had to tell us that the subject was off-limits. We knew. It was something that stayed in the background. Almost every Vietnamese family had people missing, lost, left "back there." Long before I knew what trauma, or therapy, or stigma were, I learned that not talking was the way we were supposed to deal with things. Better not to ask, and not to know.

———

In 1985, when I was in fifth grade, my mother sent a letter to my dad. He told me and my sister about it, and it was startling to hear her mentioned, a subject that I had thought would remain in permanent shadow. He said that she had come to America. My sister and I saw the envelope—the neat script-like handwriting of the return address of Swarthmore, Pennsylvania—but we never saw the letter, which must have been in Vietnamese, a language neither of us could read. I don't think either of us even asked what it said, or wondered how she had our address. It just happened that one day we learned exactly where our mother was in the world.

My dad and stepmom said we could make cards to send to our mother, but it was best to wait until we were older to meet her. Anh and I did not object; again, we did not ask questions, or wonder aloud why we were getting any of this information. Our mother was an abstraction, and maybe we were fine keeping her like that. Even then I understood that my dad could have just as easily not said anything at all. In our household he and my stepmom had absolute authority and I rarely dared to disobey them outright. So Anh and I made cards out of pieces of construction paper folded in half. We drew on them what we always drew—hills, mountains, trees, and flowers that we had personally never seen. Then we waited for a response. Waited for information. We lived in quiet, shared suspense. But after a while, after no response came, we went back to forgetting. And that's truly what it was, because mostly I forgot that I had a(nother) mother out there. I didn't know her, so I didn't know what it was, really, to miss her.

We all went back to the way things were, which was pretending like my mother didn't really exist. It wasn't hard. Sometimes I think my sister and I didn't ask questions be-cause we knew that whatever we would learn would alter us and maybe we didn't want that just yet. Or maybe we knew that it wouldn't alter us. That we would go on as we were no matter what.

It was troublesome enough being Vietnamese in our con-servative white town. There was already so much to conceal from our white friends, so many ways to pretend that we

17

were just like them. I used to look back and think it was odd that friends didn't ask us about our mother, but after I had kids of my own I understood: most children accept, or are trained to accept, the circumstances they're given. Only my few close friends ever asked where my "real" mother was. I would answer that she and my dad had gotten divorced, though I had no idea, and that she still lived in Vietnam.

I wouldn't meet my mother until almost ten years after that letter arrived. I would learn that she had written it from a women's housing center in Pennsylvania, and from there had found refugee resettlement in Boston. I would learn that she and my dad had in fact never been married. That she had our address because he had written to her in Saigon. I would learn that she had a then-twenty-year-old daughter and teenage son, and that they were all able to come to the United States because her son was, as people said back then, "Amerasian"; his father had been a white American soldier. It would help to think of my mother, retroactively, as being less alone those years in Vietnam. Less abandoned, maybe, because she had other kids—a whole other life.

In real life, telling this story is still uncomfortably dramatic. Because people always want it to be more dramatic. Because I didn't, really, think about my mother. I had curiosity, sometimes, but not longing. Because I never questioned my dad. I didn't demand to know what had happened to my mother, didn't ask about Vietnam, didn't try to see that letter she had sent, didn't ask if she'd ever responded to the homemade cards. Just like how I didn't ask why, for years, he kept two broken-down cars in the driveway along with a motorboat that he never once used. Why every drawer in the house turned into a junk drawer. There was a closet where we simply threw things—old magazines, chewed-up dog toys—and slammed the door shut. Better not to look.

———

When I was pregnant with my first child, I would sometimes wonder what childbirth had been like for my mother. Pregnancy books say that your mother's experiences can predict your own. I had a feeling that if I asked her about that, if I found her phone number and called her right up and asked, she would've said she didn't remember, because that's how she answered so many questions. But I never called. I never would have called. At the time, I hadn't seen her in maybe three years.

To be a mother is to form a new understanding of time. It is to form a new relationship with all that you know about your body and its capacities. It is not a do-over of your own childhood, but close enough.

When my children were babies, I was awake so often at two and three and four in the morning, hours I had always felt were the most mournful. In the beginning, especially, during the intense blur of regular, at times near-constant breastfeeding. When our first son was born, my husband and I were living in Chicago, on the seventh floor of a thirty-story building. Sometimes at three in the morning I would nurse and look out at the other buildings nearby, counting the lit-up windows. I would decide that within each of those windows was another mother, nursing or cleaning or somehow taking care, and that we all shared a silent connection through our various windows, our various lights.

I have always hated being up at the hour of the street sweepers. I have never cared to hear the earliest birds start their songs. I don't want to see the sky turning toward day. Being a mother has meant learning time as a function of my children's sleeping and waking. When we slept next to each other, they would often turn to me, to my body, for milk. I would wake up just enough to be aware, enough to stay afloat in a near-dream state. Often I didn't even open my eyes. I knew my children by heart. The normal measuring of the hours—traffic, sunrise—seemed an affront, a demand to return to the outside world where who you are might be someone else entirely.

And sometimes in my half-awake state I would imagine the story that my mother had told me the first time we met, in Boston, when I was nineteen years old: weeks after the fall of Saigon, she said, she had traveled across the city, from her own mother's house, to see my sister and me, her two youngest children, at our grandmother Noi's house. She had looked for open windows. Sometimes I wonder if she sensed before she got there that the house would be empty. A neighbor told her that my dad had left word: we were going to try for America. For a long time, that's all she knew. I have no idea when she heard from my dad next. One day my mother had four children in Saigon and the next day two of them were gone.

———

I met my mother the summer after my second year of college. I'd had a chance the year before, with my sister, brother, dad, and stepmom, who had all driven east together to see Cape Cod and Boston. I had declined to join them, using my receptionist job as an excuse. In truth, I was afraid: of the awkwardness, of the audience. I'd had years to prepare, but I wasn't ready. After all the years of silence, I didn't know how to manage the suddenness of my dad and stepmom saying they were going to visit my mother, like it was no big deal. The only reason I ended up seeing her at all was because I had to go to Boston for a wedding.

Here is where I confess that I have forgotten what happened when I met my mother. In my mind, I step free of the revolving doors of the suburban hotel where I was staying and I know that the woman standing some distance away can only be my mother. I know because we are the same size, same height, and she stands there looking both small and determined in a way that makes me wonder if this is how people see me. She walks toward me and the first thing she says is, You are so late. The late-summer sunlight is fierce and the doors of that hotel keep turning. I see all of this, I have written this, with the clarity of certainty that that is how it happened.

In reality, my half sister and her husband and their two young kids were waiting for me in a maroon-colored Plymouth Sundance, which looked just like the ones I had driven during high school driver's ed classes. I got into the car and we went to their apartment complex, where my mother opened the door and finally saw me. Look at you, she said, smiling. You're late. Almost twenty years I wait, and you're late.

We piled back into the car and went in search of dim sum in Chinatown. For a while we could busy ourselves with directions and parking, and then the carts laden with dumplings, and looking out for favorites, especially the rice noodle rolls filled with shrimp. We talked about school and work, and what we liked to eat, and all the Big Dig construction going on in Boston. It turned out that my mother had been working, of all places, at an envelope factory.

It also turned out that my dad and stepmom had been in communication with her over the years, sending money and packages and sometimes pictures. My mother said that my stepmom was a good lady. I'm very thankful, she said.

Afterward my mother and I walked around Chinatown while the others went on ahead. We browsed shops and I pretended to admire all the jade and gold jewelry. She insisted on buying me a Buddha-shaped moon cake. It was a food I kept trying to like but never could. I would end up bringing the moon cake all the way back to college with me before throwing it away. I tried to ask a couple of questions about Vietnam, my birth, my sister's birth, but my mother didn't say anything that counted as an answer. *That was so long ago* was her stance, and is still. How was she supposed to remember things?

Now, nearly thirty years after that first meeting, I see her point. I know what happened that day because I wrote it down. But my mind has insisted on another version. An edited, efficient scene, with those revolving hotel doors. It feels like the actual truth, which scares me. Like my mother, I am less and less sure of what is real, what is remembered, what is necessary to believe.

When I tell people about meeting my mother—only when needed, when an explanation seems required—I say that my Boston mother and I are not close, which is true. It is hard to describe how this entire arc has happened, how all of this has come to be. How distance creates distance. We saw each other; we said good-bye; we went back to our regularly scheduled lives. I know, it's disappointing sometimes, how straightforward it is, how after all, it wasn't difficult. I saw it then and I see it still. How once you are gone, it gets easier to stay gone.

———

Here is a timeline that I have pieced together:

Sometime in the late 1960s, my mother had her first child, my half sister. For many years, I didn't know who her father was, or what the circumstances of that relationship were. No one ever said, and I never asked.

Sometime in the early 1970s, my mother had another child, my half brother, who is half-white, born of a brief relationship with a white American.

Neither my mother nor my dad has ever said much about how or when they met. But they stayed together, or stayed enough together, to have two children: my sister Anh in 1973 and me in 1974.

Whatever my parents meant to each other I do not know, and wouldn't be mine to say. What I do know, what my mother has told me, is that by the spring of 1975 they weren't together. She was living with her mother and he was living with his, on the other side of the river. My sister Anh and I, it seems, were shared between them, or rather, between her and our grandmother Noi. These are the unknown hours and months I had with my mother, the ones before memory or recognition.

Those times when my dad was in the mood to tell stories about Vietnam? If I saw the right moment, if I had a burst of bravery, I would ask him what had happened to my mother. Once, he said that she had gotten lost in the crowd after an explosion. Another time, he said the bridges between her mother's house and Noi's house had been destroyed; another time, guards wouldn't let her pass. The simpler story—that there was no time or way to make another choice—makes so much more sense. But I get, now, how the mind grasps for other versions. It's a matter of distance, of safekeeping.

Over the years I have also pieced together stories about April 29 from my dad, my uncles, my grandmother Noi, and my mother. What is known is that Anh and I were with Noi, our dad, and two uncles. My third uncle had already left the country, though we wouldn't know that until he happened to find us at the refugee camp in Guam. My dad and his brothers had all agreed that if they found a way out they would take it. In Saigon, it was quickly becoming too late. A twenty-four-hour curfew was in place. The temperature hovered over one hundred degrees. North Vietnamese forces were shelling the airport, moving into the city. My grandmother said it was time to go. Weeks later, when my mother could get to Noi's house, she found it empty. As she says to me every time, no one even left a note.

———

When my kids finally met my mother, my older son had just turned eight and my younger son would soon turn six. I planned the trip to Boston through my dad, who called my mother and let her know that we would be visiting. I booked a hotel near the Public Garden, thinking my kids would enjoy the swan boats, but didn't tell them why we were there. To them it was just a jaunt from New York, where we'd been staying for one of my teaching gigs. At the time, our home was in northern California, and for years that distance had been an easy excuse for not seeing my mother.

On the morning of the visit, a steady rain began as my kids and I walked to the nearest T stop. We hurried down the steps, purchased our fares, then lingered by the map, watching trains come and go. We were on the Green Line, the oldest subway in America, and my kids were fascinated, as I had been years ago on my first trip to this city, by the individual streetcars skidding along the embedded tracks. My children were delighted by the old-fashionedness, how people had to climb up into the cars rather than board from a platform. Quickly the boys memorized the system—which train letters corresponded with which destinations—because that's what they liked to do. We often took train and subway rides for fun, with no real destination.

I had been putting off telling them where we were going in case she canceled, though I also knew that if she were to cancel I wouldn't know; she simply wouldn't be at home, wouldn't show, like that time my older son was one year old. At Park Street we changed to the Red Line and I pointed out our stop. When they asked why, I told them, Because we're going to visit my mother—your other grandmother.

Oh, Michigan grandma is here? my older son asked. That's what he and his brother, of their own devising, have always called my stepmom. They have a Michigan grandma and a Michigan grandpa, and, through their father, a DC grandma and a DC grandpa. Geography, it seems, defines us all.

Not Michigan grandma, I said. Your other grandma, the one you haven't met yet. My mother.

You have another mother? My older child often ends up speaking for both him and his brother, a habit that is difficult for all of us to break.

Yes, I said. You know how I was born in Vietnam? Well, when we left, my mother didn't come with us; she came

27

here later on and she lives here in Boston. So we're going to visit her.

My children knew the story of how my family had left as refugees, but I'd always avoided the part about my mother staying behind. I guess I thought it was too much for them to handle. In hindsight, I realize I was just replicating the silence I'd been taught. Of course it had been easier for my dad to say nothing; it was easier for me, too.

My son looked at me with thoughtful curiosity, familiar since his baby days. The child who would gaze at every person in a room.

So, he said, we have another grandmother?

Yes, I said. Exactly.

It was midmorning on a Saturday in June, and our outbound train was mostly empty. The man sitting near us was clearly listening, with great interest, to everything I was saying to my children. I couldn't blame him.

My younger son, who was less of a worrier than his brother, smiled and said, We're going to visit Boston grandma!

Yes, I said.

Oh, okay, my older son said, the way he does when I tell him what's for dinner and he has no objection.

My children looked out at the grayness of the day and the grayness of the Charles River—they love it when transportation must make use of bridges—and we didn't say much more until the train arrived at the station. I met the eye of the man who'd been listening to our conversation and he nodded a little, which I interpreted as *good luck*.

From the T station we took a car to the sprawling apartment complex where my Boston mother has lived since her arrival in the 1980s. All of the buildings look the same, and over the years she has moved from one apartment to another without ever really leaving. It was still raining when we got out of the car and walked toward what I thought was the correct building. We tried to huddle under an awning while I checked my phone to make sure I had the right address, then walked to the next building, which was also wrong. Finally I called my mother's number. We almost never spoke on the phone, so I was surprised when she answered.

Where are you? she said. Supposed to be here by now.

We're here, I said, but I can't find the right building.

She tried to give me walking directions, but I couldn't explain where we were exactly, and soon the kids and I were standing in the middle of the parking lot.

Then I saw her: a woman with a fuchsia umbrella, waving to us from a curb near the farthest apartment building.

There she is, I said to my kids.

We got to her and she called out, Hiiii, to my children, saying, Give Grandma a hug! She held out her arms and they both went into them, hugging her as if they already knew who she was.

I wondered how it could be that she looked exactly the same as I remembered her: delicate frame, thin skin around her eyes. She wore a woolen houndstooth coat and satiny heels and a jade and gold necklace and the kind of flowy pants that my grandmother also wore, that I associate with all Vietnamese women of a certain age, that I sometimes think of as waiting for me, too.

———

My sister says that our relationship with our mother only goes one way. We're the ones who have to visit, who have to call, who have to do everything, she says. If we don't then we never hear from her.

This is true. And yet.

We are the ones who left her. Even if it wasn't our choice. We left; we are the leavers. And we don't even regret it because we are glad to have grown up in America because it is what we know.

I say to my sister, Maybe we are the ones who must make amends.

What I don't say to my sister: Maybe we are the ones

who, knowing we can never make amends enough, can never do enough, can never apologize in any way to make a difference—maybe because of this we keep leaving. We get so used to that feeling of being gone that it's so much harder to imagine returning.

Maybe it was easier when we didn't know the truth.

It was easier when we didn't ask questions.

———

In America, in my mother's one-bedroom apartments, the window blinds are always drawn and partly broken, the altar for Buddha and the ancestors is the focal point of the living room, and there are piles, everywhere, of what someone else might call clutter. In this apartment, she had spread a blanket on the floor and covered it with an assortment that my kids found delightful: stacks of paper napkins printed with a casino logo, boxes of tea, plastic containers, tin buckets and mixing bowls, mini water bottles, an open box of hairbrushes and toiletries, a plastic bag filled with other plastic bags, a kitchen scale.

Right away my older son asked, What is all this for?

Things I need, she said.

For what?

For this and for that, she said.

This is how she has always answered questions, and I

remembered how when I first met her I asked her to tell me the story of how she met my dad and she said, Oh, who can remember.

Now that my kids had truly met my mother and we were in her apartment, I didn't know what to do next. She seemed content to sit on her pink sofa, so we all sat down. When I asked what she usually did with her days, she said, This. We sit here; we relax. She smiled at her boyfriend, who was texting on his phone.

Did I mention her boyfriend? In truth, I'd forgotten about him. As my mother explained it, he was Chinese and spoke very little English and no Vietnamese, and she was Vietnamese and spoke decent English but no Chinese. Over the years, she had learned enough Chinese to communicate with him.

Has he learned Vietnamese, or more English? I asked her. She laughed.

I asked how long they'd been together and she said, More than ten years. Actually, she said, we're married. He's my husband.

Oh, I said. When did you get married?

Years ago. I never told your daddy; I don't know why.

My mother was eager to give my kids bottles of mango juice, which they happily accepted as treats. We continued to sit on the pink sofa. We took pictures of each other. I peeked into the small kitchen but didn't go in. My mother kept asking my kids if they wanted something to eat, but my kids were far more interested in the piles on the floor—the paper napkins, the scale. To amuse themselves, they started weighing various items around them.

I tried to make conversation with my mother. I asked questions I'd asked before. Do you remember anything about the day I was born, or when my sister was born?

Not really.

Are you going to visit Vietnam again soon? She'd spent months there last year and would probably go again in the winter.

What's Vietnam like now and what was it like back then?

Oh, so very different.

I asked about my half brother; I asked about my half sister and her kids. Where were they? What were they doing? I had all this family that didn't seem like mine, stretched out across Boston, across the United States, across the world in Vietnam.

We talked about the pictures of her parents she had set on the altar. It needed dusting, and next to plates of fruit and incense, candles and fake flowers, my mother had also left champagne glasses filled with rolls of Life Savers and mini bottles of whiskey.

She lived a long time, my mother said, of her own mother. Age ninety-something. You remember her?

I did. I had met her once, nearly twenty years earlier when Noi and I had traveled to Vietnam, the one and only time so far that I've been there since leaving as a refugee baby. Somehow my dad had arranged for me to visit my maternal grandmother in her home in Saigon. I can still see her as she was, shawl draped around her shoulders, teeth stained from betel nut. We sat on a cushionless wooden sofa. We had not been able to communicate much and I hadn't stayed long, but we had smiled and stared at each other over cups of tea.

As always, I didn't know what to say in the presence of my mother—in the presence of so much that was here and gone in the same room, same moment. We were selves who didn't mesh and didn't match. We didn't know each other at all. Our histories had separated long ago and had never truly met again.

My mother was getting agitated by my kids' determination to weigh anything they could find on that scale, so they stopped and wandered off into her bedroom. She had plastic storage boxes all around the room, filled with shoes and makeup, and an open closet that revealed a tight row of dresses and jackets. The bed was layered with clothes. I wondered if I had gotten my own messy, keep-everything tendencies from her, or if this was a consequence of refugee-ness: having as much as possible nearby, just in case.

My mother shooed the children out of her room and

they went back to the pink sofa. There wasn't anything else to do. We'd been there less than an hour, but it was clear the visit was over. The boyfriend, now husband, stood up. My mother asked my kids if they wanted to take more mango juice with them.

Bye-bye, she said when my kids had put on their shoes. She gave them another hug and they gave her another hug. Bye, they said. Everyone was smiling. She patted their heads and said they were good boys, handsome boys, and told me to send pictures in the mail. Sure, I said, though I was also pretty sure I wouldn't get around to what sometimes felt like insurmountable logistics: printing pictures, finding the address, getting an envelope and a stamp, all the work it would take to put something in the actual mailbox.

As far as I knew, my mother had never replied to the homemade cards that my sister and I had sent in response to the letter she had written, back in 1985. We never wrote her again. But she had old photos of us from back then because of the packages my dad and stepmom had sent without ever telling us. There I was at ten years old in a striped dress I had loved, my tortoiseshell glasses crooked on my face, and there was my sister with too much hairspray in her bangs, and we were together with our mother's other children, all of us in a basket near her front door.

Byyyye, my kids said again. They waved. My mother and

her husband waved back. My kids and I left the apartment building and stood outside—it had stopped raining—waiting for a car to take us back to the subway station.

The kids were in good moods, happy to get back on a train. They seemed to have simply accepted the fact of another grandmother and now their attention was on what was next: lunch, more transportation. They did not know what I was thinking, which was that I am always leaving my mother.

———

I have tried to imagine my children leaving me—leaving as in disappearing without a note, fleeing to a different part of the world, and being gone for years. When my children were babies, I would hold them, study them sometimes, and try to imagine it. When my children were each eight months old, the age I was when my family became refugees, I tried to imagine it. I keep trying, imagining, because it feels impossible. Unbearable to think of my children having no memory, no imprint, of me.

Is it better, lucky even, that my sister and I were too young for memory, too young for imagery? We might have left in fear, we might have cried, but we have no memory of this. Whatever was retained returns in other ways—vague anxieties, alternating moments of recklessness and caution—but we don't have the active pain my mother must have had, must have still, even if she will never speak of it.

My mother is not an emotional person. She is no-nonsense. She is a wave of the hand—Eh, who can remember how things were? She is not one to tell stories. She resists the very idea of a narrative. Maybe because this is a story that no one would want. But I suppose we just don't get to choose. We must contend. I am trying to contend.

———

Here's what happened, that time in Boston when my older son was a year old and my mother didn't show up to meet him: her daughter, my half sister, showed up instead. She explained about the casino. The way she said it, it sounded like a necessity, a fact of life. Our mother had to go to Fox-woods, you see. Then she gave me an envelope—a gift from all of us, she said. I knew it was money. We're Vietnamese; there was a new baby; money was going to be in an envelope. I didn't want to accept, but even as I protested I knew I had no choice.

My half sister only stayed a few minutes. She admired the baby. She was in a hurry because of parking, she said.

She left and that was that. I looked at the envelope in my hand. Inside was a couple hundred dollars.

I'm not sure I ever expected my mother to show up. I wasn't hurt, wasn't surprised. If I ever feel bitterness toward her, it is so fleeting that it leaves only a slight impression, an almost-ness that doesn't take shape. Always I think: I have no right to want anything or expect anything from her.

After all, my mother didn't know me. Why would she need to know my children? She had children and grand-children already. They were her actual life, the daily being together around a table, eating and laughing and watching the same television. These have become the memories of how they have lived out, are living out, their years. I'm not there. My sister isn't there. My children aren't there. We aren't in each other's thoughts. It's the people who are there in front of you who get to be your actual life.

———

Mothers aren't supposed to take up so much space. They're supposed to do the work—quietly, efficiently, and behind the scenes—and then get out of the way. This is the message I have always seen, on shows and in movies and all over real life, and now get to experience. The dismissal, the disdain. I feel it most when I have the urge to tell someone I'm not just a mother and then recognize what I have internalized in even thinking that phrase, *just a mother*.

One day at my older son's school, I had to identify my-self and instead of saying I'm a mother I said, I'm a parent. I don't remember the circumstances or why this needed to be stated, but as I spoke I saw the words in front of me: *I'm apparent.* And I was. I wasn't *just* anything. I had become, in parenthood, apparent to myself in a way that I was not before—a way that was so intense, I knew I would spend the rest of my life turning it over in my mind, trying to understand it. Instead of slipping into the background, being the coordinator of all things who then hurries out of view, I was the opposite: I was present; I was here. I was being seen— at least, by myself.

———

As I write this, it has been four years since my children have seen their Boston grandmother and I don't know when they will see her again. We live an airplane ride away, which is both an impediment and an excuse. Boston requires advance planning; it's not a vacation, but it is an expense. And for what? An hour or two with a family that is mine by DNA but not by time? Is it terrible to say that—to think that?

Sometimes I feel like if I don't make the effort to see my mother and family in Boston we will never see each other again because, so far, this has been true. We aren't estranged, just separate. But I now know the strange secret of this: absence gets easier, not harder.

And if nothing happens, who will care? My sister tells me that I'm the only one who cares. She thinks I am making this circumstance of life more difficult than it is. That sometimes families are made rather than given.

Perhaps it's true that I am bothered by the narrative mess and messiness of my family's story, which, like all family stories, can never have a resolution. I see myself trying to fix the messiness through my own mothering, right down to chaperoning field trips and sewing tae kwon do badges. The concreteness of mothering, I think, surely will affix me to their lives and memories. Because a foundational truth of parenthood is that you're raising a child for the rest of *their* lives. Not for yourself. The point of raising a child is to let them leave. To help them leave. Because they will leave; they must.

In the middle of the night, the hour or two before the street sweepers, I think about how so much of my life hearkens back to a time that I can't remember and didn't choose: that time I left my mother in Vietnam, and didn't know or see her until I was nineteen years old. There is no returning, no repairing. Every mother knows that motherhood is all about time, about waiting and watching. The days are long but the years are short, people keep saying to me. Complete strangers on playgrounds, at restaurants. Only other parents would say such a thing. My relationship with my children is also my relationship with time, with the concept of motherhood, with the mothers I have known, with the mother I have never known. It is a catch in the throat. It is the edge of tears.

It is wanting to be here, in this moment, so that I will stay in my children's minds. We cannot control what our children will remember, what they won't. We are always hedging our bets against the future.

Before I go to sleep, I check on my children. This is a universal thing that parents are known to do. Sometimes it is very late and I do that parent thing of standing in the doorway or sitting on the edge of the bed to watch the children sleep. What are we doing when we do this? We're checking to make sure they're literally alive, for one thing. We're checking to make sure they're not sleeping half on the floor, because we know they sometimes contort themselves hilariously. We're checking to make sure they're comfortable with their blankets and pillows and stuffies. We're making sure that they are safe as we understand the idea of safe, which is to say within reach of us. Sometimes all I want is this: to be in the same room, at the same time, together. A brief thing I can know as true. At such times, in darkness, I can't help thinking about how far our bodies have traveled, will travel. What we go through to get here, to remain, to stay. Sometimes I feel like I'm just shoring up these moments of being a mother. Like it's insurance, because to be a mother is to be in a vague, permanent state of fear of loss. So, just in case, I want them to know I was there. Here. I wanted to be. I never wanted to leave.

DATE OF BIRTH

Like a lot of refugees and immigrants in the United States, I have two birthdays, a legal one and a "real" one. My dad once said that he got the paperwork wrong, that he'd remembered the months but not the days my sister and I were born. Because birthdays didn't really matter in Vietnam, or at least they didn't used to. Instead, aging was measured by Tet, the lunar new year. Everyone moving forward at the same time. In Vietnam, the date of your death means more than the date of your birth.

Of all the things I could have envied about my non-Vietnamese friends when I was growing up, one of the biggest was that they could document their births down to the minute. No one in my refugee family even had a birth certificate. I would never know such details—what I thought of as facts—about myself, and it would be many years before I would find something that would feel like evidence, like proof, of my beginnings.

———

It's a Vietnamese custom to celebrate the first birthday because if you make it that far, your chance of survival is strong. Twelve objects are placed around the child and whichever one the child goes for—pencil, ruler, money—is supposed to represent their future. After my first son was born, I asked my dad if my sister Anh and I had had this kind of ceremony and, if so, what objects had we chosen? He had no recollection. Only later did it occur to me that my August birthday would have happened not long after our resettlement in Michigan. I am ashamed, still, to think of this. When I look at the few pictures we have of those early years, I see my sister and me surrounded by toys from our sponsor's church bins. We often rode our tricycles inside the house. We are usually smiling, having no idea what everything actually cost.

The first birthday that stays in my mind is Anh's, the year she turned five. We were living in a drafty rental house that our sponsor had found for us, the place where we spent our first few years in America. That house returns to me, often, in dreams. The scarring in the old hardwood floors. How every day seemed like winter even when wild roses bloomed along the chain-link fence in the backyard. Whenever I go back to Grand Rapids I drive past this house, staring in wonder at the now-bright paint, the now-coolness of the neighborhood.

For Anh's birthday we had new dresses, she in red velveteen, me in pale yellow dotted swiss. Even though it's March, we wore ankle socks instead of tights. We both opened presents, and someone took pictures. These images have become my memories now. The gleam of the wrapping paper, printed with multicolored squares, takes me right back to that moment. We even have a store-bought layer cake with a candle in the shape of the number 5. Anh makes a face at the cake, the camera. I laugh to see it now, but I also see the tension. There's my grandmother's teacup, my dad's can of beer, a canister of Pringles, an ashtray ready for cigarettes. There's my future stepsister nearby, a few years older, already tired of this whole thing. My dad is smiling, but we already know how fast his temper turns. When I look at these pictures, I wonder what everyone was thinking. Was this what birthday parties were? How were we supposed to know what everything meant?

I keep an adjacent memory of my new stepmom asking

me if I wanted a different birth date. We were sitting at a kitchen table and she said that no one knew for sure what my birthday really was, so I could pick any day I wanted to celebrate it. The concept was wild to me. Lawless. I didn't recognize that my stepmom was trying to give me something—a sense of freedom, maybe. I don't remember what I answered. Maybe nothing, because I was often too scared or shy to say anything at all.

At some point—was it years later?—my grandmother Noi decided that my birthday was actually August 31 and that Anh's birthday was March 2, a week or two off from our legal birth dates. Because Noi said it, I went with it. Anh took the liberty of alternating between her two dates, and over the years I saw that it was up to us to decide what real meant, and who would get to know it. Instead of birth certificates we had permanent resident cards that were literally green, with the words *resident alien* on them. As we reached age eighteen, we would each apply for U.S. citizenship and eventually receive certificates of naturalization that would allow us to get U.S. passports—ultimate proof of identity. I had no clue that birth certificates were a twentieth-century development, implemented as a measure of statistical record, and often used as an anti-immigration tactic to figure out who was and was not from the U.S. It didn't occur to me, at all, to question the strangeness of being a living person having to prove that you had been born.

Not long after Anh's fifth birthday, my stepmom moved us all to a ranch house on Florence Street, on the southeastern side of the city. Our neighbors were mostly white, some who kept their distance and others who made a show of keeping their lawns mowed in the summer and driveways shoveled in the winter. My sister and new stepsister and newborn half brother and I became siblings, settling into a place where we would learn about Doritos and Little Debbie snack cakes, Brownie troop and Barbie dolls and board games with names like Pay Day and Hungry Hungry Hippos. I spent a lot of time observing my white friends' bologna sandwiches and how their mothers must have ironed the Peter Pan collars of their blouses. We ate sweetened cereal every morning and my grandmother's stews and curries every night, and we lived for television and its commercials. I learned, as so many of us refugees and first-generation immigrants did, the unspoken nuances of isolation. The world of friends and school and American life that existed outside our house felt like real, actual life, and entering into it meant a careful folding up of the self. I became a self-conscious, quiet child trying to figure out and memorize the way the rest of the world worked.

———

The year I turned ten I had my first and, still to this day, only real birthday party where friends were invited. The planning gave me anxiety for weeks because I was afraid that no one would come or that they'd have a terrible time. I was haunted by a chapter in *Little Women* in which Amy plans a fancy party, complete with lobster salad, but only one girl shows up. And I fretted that our house, a little more run-down than the others in our neighborhood, would never be good enough. One friend had had a birthday in a McDonald's playroom where the chairs were shaped like toadstools and everybody got free Happy Meals. This could hardly be topped, not even by another friend's party at Chi-Chi's, a Tex-Mex restaurant that relied on dim lighting, endless free chips and salsa, and waitresses who wore flouncy off-the shoulder dresses. My parents did not believe that birthdays were worth spending money on, especially since there were so many of us and the day rolled around every damn year. I understood this. I felt no excitement about turning ten. It was just something that happened because time said so. The worry I felt about the party was like being called on in class: the fear of everyone turning to stare. But I had learned early on that there were a lot of things one had to endure in order to be viewed as American.

For my birthday party, Anh and I blew up balloons and taped them to crepe streamers we hung around the living room. My stepmom suggested we plan games, like guessing how many pebbles were in a glass bowl, with a candy bar as the prize. I was in charge of the cake. I had learned to make Duncan Hines and Betty Crocker mixes because my stepmom, in an effort to keep me occupied after school, had enrolled me in a cake-decorating class at a community education center. There, surrounded by older women, I had learned how to turn buttercream icing into roses, leaves, and borders of unbroken waves.

I made a chocolate sheet cake—devil's food, the box called it—because that was the only kind of baking pan we had, and decorated it like I was drawing on construction paper, piping a frosting unicorn in a field of flowers. I edged the cake in pale green flourishes and wrote *Happy Birthday* in even script. I did this under my grandmother Noi's watch, and partly because she was watching. She did almost all the cooking in our household but didn't care for sweets or baking. To her, the oven was a storage space. She seemed interested, though, in my intentions, and I think she found the whole thing amusing in the way that she found most American customs amusing.

My friends arrived on time to the party. We played games and my stepmom brought out sloppy Joes, potato chips, and 7Up. Then we gathered around the sheet cake with its ten candles and I smiled for the camera and the one picture my parents have of this day. I'm wearing my favorite purple shirt and my glasses are, as usual, a little bit crooked. I don't remember opening gifts or guessing how many rocks were in the bowl, or eating the cake. I just remember feeling immense gratitude and relief that nothing had gone too terribly, and that the day soon would be over.

———

By the time my dad turned forty, almost five years later, I was making birthday cakes for everyone in the family. This time, my stepmom said I needed to make a special, secret cake shaped like a hill, with *Over the Hill* written in icing. I had a limited grasp of idioms and asked, What hill? For a long time after, I pictured my dad bicycling up a craggy mountain and swaying at the top, not ready to go downward.

I made two cakes, molding part of one into a hemisphere that could sit on the sheet cake. I covered the hill with little green frosting rosettes, for grass. I used a fine-tip nozzle to write *Over the Hill* and *Happy Birthday Dad!*

When we brought out the whole thing, my dad did not laugh. I'll always remember the look on his face. He understood the idiom. He was forty years old—to me, then, that really did seem old—and he was not ready. My stepmom led us all in singing "Happy Birthday," but I knew that my dad was unhappy and later there might be consequences. He didn't want the cake, the day, that green hill. He was a Vietnamese man in Michigan, a refugee always, someone who had never left where he'd been re-settled, who talked about traveling but never did. At forty there was no turning back from this life he had made, the life that had happened. What had he signed up for? Who gets to decide?

My mother in Boston, it turned out, didn't care about birth-days either. When I met her that first time, when I was nine-teen, and we walked around Chinatown and talked about weather and construction, and how a major highway that currently cut through the city would one day be submerged, and how important it was to get good grades and how im-portant education, in general, was, I had to work up the nerve to ask what she could tell me about when and where I was born, and what that had been like for her. My dad and Noi could only ever say that I was born in a hospital. Forget about the recording of time, or weight, or length. But my mother didn't remember either. I have asked her almost every time I've visited her in the years since, as if she'll suddenly recall. She always looks at me as if to say, What difference does it make?

Who knows? she said, with a little laugh, the last time I saw her in Boston. It was part dismissal but also fact. Another time she said, Why does it matter? You're here now.

———

The thing about having a baby, a nurse said to a group of us in a childbirth class, back when I was pregnant with my first son, is that only one person needs to show up. We all sort of laughed at that, but it also felt like another reminder of how responsible a mother must be, has to be. Every time someone talked about *expecting* as in "expecting a child," as in "what to expect when you're expecting," I would think about the hidden demands encoded in that word.

Both of my kids were born in Chicago, though at the time my husband and I were based in a small college town two hours away. It wasn't just about the health care, or the unusually generous insurance. (A year after my second son was born, right before we moved to California, I drove by the college town hospital and saw that it was in the process of being demolished.) I wanted my kids to be able to say *I was born in Chicago* for the rest of their lives. And they do. It is a statement that requires no additional explanation. It feels like a relief to know exactly when my children were born, to have copies of their birth certificates, to have photos of their first minutes in this world, as if such facts could never be lost, never be altered.

Maybe my dad forgot when my sister and I were born because he didn't think he would need to know. Maybe he forgot because that's part of what he had to do in order to leave his home, his country. Once, when I saw my mother in Boston, after college, she said, Everything was such a long time ago. She does not know or remember my birthday and I could not tell you hers.

In the United States, the significance of an individual birthday didn't even matter as much before nineteenth-century industrialization, when the push to align clocks and timetables made everyone more aware of their own passage through time.

I am always on the lookout for dual-birthday people. Because that is more than coincidence. It's a history of migration and displacement. It's diasporic. A sometimes secret harboring of selves.

My grandmother Noi died on December 21, 2007. Winter solstice. She was eighty-seven years old, having been born, she had told us, in 1920. After she died—aortic dissection, swift—I couldn't remember if we had ever talked about the subject of death. I guess I had thought she would never die. As far as I knew, she had no fears. Not that she was fearless, but that she wasn't guided by fear, not the way I was. She had never spent a night in a hospital, had never been seriously ill. In my last memories of her alive, she is standing on her tiptoes to water one of her many hanging plants.

Since her death, my family has tried to gather in Michigan every year to commemorate the date. We make a ton of food—cha gio, banh xeo—and light candles and incense. We celebrate. Drink too much wine and cognac, play board games, sing karaoke. In her lifetime, Noi did not have birthday parties for herself. In her death, she has a party nearly every year.

I was in Chicago the night Noi died. My stepmom called, waking me up, and I drove to Michigan just ahead of the blizzard that would cover Grand Rapids, the city where Noi had settled and never really left. Family friends from all around the area, members of the temple my grandmother had been part of, people from the Vietnamese community that had grown into the thousands over the years, came to my parents' house, where my grandmother lay in her coffin, in accordance with Buddhist custom, to pay respects. For two days, people brought tea and gifts and company. We, the family, wore white cloths around our heads to signify our mourning. It felt deeply right to have Noi there, to see her, to know she was nearby.

But then we had to let her go. Often I recall the barely plowed road we drove, and the fields of heavy snow, on the way to the crematory. It was a building somewhere out in the country, and we stood in a space that looked like an industrial garage. There was a button to press, to begin the cremation, and we all had to decide who would do it. Finally we decided it would be a group of grandchildren, all at once, a shared responsibility.

A day later, my sister and I looked through the photo albums Noi had kept in her bedroom at my uncle's house, where she'd been living for the past ten years while helping to raise his son. She'd had these albums since the seventies and eighties, the pictures yellowed from their time spent in plastic. She stored them in a drawer of a credenza, where we found a small box that I hadn't seen before. It held her few pieces of gold and jade jewelry and more photos— black-and-whites with scalloped edges, taken in Vietnam. People, possibly relatives, I would never recognize.

At the bottom of this box: two whisper-thin pieces of

paper. Tear-off pages from one-a-day calendars written in Vietnamese and French. One said March 2. The other, August 31. On the back of mine she had written my name.

Had Noi carried these with her all the way from Vietnam when we left, escaping the end of a war? Or had someone sent them to her? Why had we never seen these pages before? Had she forgotten she had them? No one can ever say. My sister and I just stared at them, at each other. All those years of wondering, answered.

It's a gift, this knowledge, but at the same time it doesn't change anything. I think Noi knew that. The years pass regardless. I haven't really celebrated my birthday since I was ten years old. The dates that stay in my mind belong to others: December 21; April 29; the days my children were born.

A few years ago, I saw a group of people celebrating a forty-seventh-birthday at a restaurant. Not a milestone birthday and maybe that's why I paid attention. It occurred to me that it was not, of course, the age that mattered but the fact of another year made, shaped, endured. Another year of being a person in this world. It is not an accomplishment, being born—that is, not our own accomplishment—but staying alive is. Somehow I had not quite grasped that concept until that moment.

My kids, like most kids I know, care very much about

their birthdays. They cannot wait to be older. On their first birthdays, they crawled toward objects that might represent their future. Maybe we all just want to hang on to one certainty, that there was a moment in which we were set into the world. It's the same need I see in classroom graffiti carved onto desks, the backs of chairs in an auditorium: *I was here. This time, this place, this life.* Happy birthday, someone says, and the person replies, Thank you. I watched that person at the restaurant smile, blow out the candles. It's a thing that happens in life that makes everyone in the room start clapping.

Of course, I took a picture of Noi's calendar pages. A picture, itself proof, of papers that have become my proof. I keep the pages in an acid-free archival box. I'm not sure what else to do with them. I have always held two birthdays in my mind. The legal one and the real one. I could be either/or. I could have a secret identity.

To this day, whenever I have to write down my date and place of birth I feel like I'm slipping into an alternate identity. Like going by one name with friends and another with my family. Like how I never say "Ho Chi Minh City"; I say "Saigon."

Maybe this slippage, this in-between, is what my grandmother was offering me. Like so many Vietnamese refugees and immigrants, she looked forward more than back. She did not talk in regrets. She didn't forget the past, but she didn't live in it either.

I try to picture my mother arriving at Noi's house in Saigon and realizing that we were gone. I try to picture my dad as he was when he understood he had to leave his own country. Not yet thirty years old, with two babies, having to start over. Every question, every thing, is about the unknown future.

What would you say, at such a moment, if someone asked a question about who you are or when you began? What would you forget, or want to forget? What would you answer?

LICH VẠN-PHƯỚC – 1973 – QUÝ-SỬU

THÁNG BA   MARS

2

THỨ SÁU   VENDREDI

Tháng Giêng (đủ) – Năm Quý-Sửu

Kiến : Giáp Dần   Ngày :

Tiết : Vũ Thủy   **28**   Đinh Dậu

Hành Hỏa – Trực Nguy (xấu) – Sao Lâu (tốt lắm)

NÊN : Dựng cửa công, cưới gả.

Ngày hạp tuổi : Kỷ-Dậu Tàu-Sửu, Đinh-Tỵ

Khắc tuổi : Quý-Dậu, Quý-Mão, Giáp-Tý, Giáp-Ngọ.
Các tuổi khác bình thường.

Giờ tốt : Tý, Sửu – Giờ kỵ : Mão, Dần.

Thiên đức (tốt).

Chuẩn-Đề Thập-Trai

Trong như ngọc, trắng như ngà.

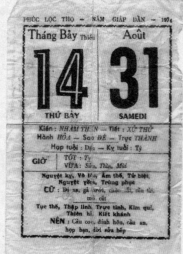

PHÚC LỘC THỌ – NĂM GIÁP DẦN – 1974

Tháng Bảy Thiếu   **Août**

14   31

THỨ BẢY   **SAMEDI**

Kiến : NHÂM THÂN – Tiết : XỬ THỬ

Hành HỎA – Sao ĐÊ – Trực THÀNH

Hợp tuổi : Dậu – Kỵ tuổi : Tỵ

GIỜ | TỐT : Tỵ
VỪA : Sửu, Thìn, Mùi

Nguyệt kỵ, Vô Hạ, Âm thổ, Tứ biệt,
Nguyệt yêm, Trùng phục

CỬ : Đi xa, gả cưới, chôn cất, đầu tời,
mổ cắt

Tục thế, Thập linh, Trực tinh, Kim quỉ,
Thiên hỉ, Kiết khánh

NÊN : Cầu con, đính hôn, cầu an,
họp bạn, dời sửa bếp

4

THE PHOTOGRAPH

I wasn't looking for the photograph of my mother when I found it. I was merely snooping, digging through boxes of receipts and scraps of electronics—so many things my dad and stepmom couldn't bear to throw away. None of your business, was one of my stepmom's standard lines. My house, my rules. I had always loved the word *snooping*. Almost innocent sounding, yet it was also a little like thievery. I had never even seen a picture of my mother before, never held one in my hands. She looked so young here, posing. Dressed up, hair done. But her face was tentative, staring instead of smiling. I stuck the picture in my pocket, then later put it in my desk, then in an envelope in a box of books that I would carry from apartment to apartment for the next two decades.

It was the summer after I had met my mother that first time. It was the mid-1990s, me on a brief visit home from college. I'm sure my dad was renovating the house because he was always renovating, drywall half-done, tiles stilled in their push across the kitchen floor. My dad and stepmom had bought this house when I was in seventh grade, and it had meant moving to a new school system in a far exurb, far enough for my stepmom to feel like she was living "out in the country," as she had wanted. Later, I would learn that she and my dad had drained all of our college savings for the down payment. But I didn't suppose there was much in those accounts anyway.

The house sat off a stretch of divided highway dotted with former farmhouses and new industrial parks. It was hidden from the road, down a long driveway that bumped over a tiny bridge and past a scummy pond banded by willow trees. My stepmom had fallen in love with all of it, especially the house itself, a cottage-like A-frame with what she grandiosely called wings on either side. Really it was just another ranch house with an awkward A wedged in the middle, shingled on the outside and paneled on the inside. My stepmom said it reminded her of a cabin in the woods, and I couldn't think why that would be a good thing. She claimed it sat on an acre of land, even though that wasn't true, because she yearned to have property. She had acre ambitions.

The printed capital letter *A* contains a window; it is a triangle on top of a trapezoid. For the next years, until my sister Anh and I went to college, we would share that part of the triangle, in a doorless room accessible by a steep set of stairs that led directly from the trapezoid living room. Some evenings, my dad and stepmom would turn off all the lights and watch an action movie, letting the volume go as loud as they wanted, pretending they were in a theater. Back then, no neighbors lived close enough to complain. But I, trying to read or sleep in the triangle, would hear every bloodletting injury happening below in the trapezoid.

To me, that house was all dankness and darkness. I had liked where we lived before, a house built into a hillside just steep enough for decent sledding in the winter. I had gotten to the point where I felt less shy around the other kids in the neighborhood, where I felt brave enough to bicycle to Gas City by myself and buy candy that I would carry in my books and eat within the shelter of climbed trees. I had no wish to be further concealed; I already felt hidden enough.

My dad and stepmom said they would redo every part of that new old house, but by the time I left for college they'd made little progress. My dad was always making plans and then abandoning them. He once hauled in clearance-priced hardwood flooring for the living room and said it would have to sit for a few weeks, to acclimate to the room temperature. But the flooring partly obstructed the view of the television, so he moved the pile to another room, where it stayed, acclimating, for the next six years.

My dad and stepmom became gradual experts in accumulation. While she scoured the clearance aisles at T.J. Maxx, stocking up on dishware and candle sets that might become Christmas gifts, my dad collected cast-off auto parts and kitchen gadgets featured in infomercials. He often had four different cars in the driveway and yard, waiting for repair. You never know what you might need, my stepmom would say; my dad would say, Almost anything can be fixed up.

—

When I was growing up, I didn't really have conversations with my dad. Sure, there was talk about schoolwork and chores, and all of us kids would get yelled at for not washing dishes or for leaving a mess somewhere. But there wasn't the kind of chat I saw on sitcoms or soap operas, where people sat around with their problems and talked about feelings. Whenever I heard my dad and uncles and grandmother talking in Vietnamese, I knew that us kids weren't supposed to be involved. My dad was not one to ask how we were doing. We didn't hug when we saw each other; we didn't give kisses good night. No one read to me before

64

bedtime and I didn't even know such a thing truly happened in other families until I went to college. Before we moved to the cottage house, before my dad quit smoking for good, I would often see him sitting outside in the cold, lighting up his Winstons. I knew better than to interrupt his solitude.

I don't mean this as a criticism of my parents. He was a refugee and she was a daughter of immigrants in a mostly white town in Michigan. They were focused on getting by, and that meant not talking about the big things: war or why we were there or what had been lost. My dad spent most of his time working or hanging out with his friends. After he lost his job at the feather factory, he tried to start a contracting business but mostly helped fix up other people's houses. He was especially skilled at tile and flooring, and we always had boxes of leftover tile in the garage. His enjoyments, as far as I knew, were eating, drinking, and going to parties. The Vietnamese community in Grand Rapids was growing, and my dad prided himself on knowing everyone. When Anh and I were little, we would go to what we called the Vietnamese parties, too, with our younger brother (our stepsister never went), and we would play in basements and yards with the other kids, all of us eventually falling asleep somewhere. I would always wake up being carried by my dad, being set into the back seat of the car next to my sister. Not long after we moved to the faraway house, my dad started going to those parties by himself.

We were not a family that ate dinner together every night. But we did watch movies. My stepmom would consult the TV schedule in the newspaper and make us gather for *Superman, Star Wars, The Sound of Music, The Day After.* I always fell asleep during the annual replay of *The Wizard of Oz*, probably to escape it. We almost never saw movies in the theater because it was too expensive and my dad always got stressed out trying to get us there. Plus, he thought most movies were boring. Too much talking, he always said. He wanted to watch on his own time, rewind action scenes in his own living room. His entire life changed with the advent of affordable VCRs.

In those days, where we lived, my dad could only get Asian movies from Saigon Market, the Vietnamese grocery that had become his second home. It was a tiny shop on 28th Street, a commercial thoroughfare of malls and chains and dealerships that cut through all of Grand Rapids. Here my dad rented Vietnamese soap dramas for Noi and what we called kung fu movies for himself. These were usually Chinese films dubbed in Vietnamese. Bruce Lee, sure, but mostly copycats. I can still hear the sounds: the guttural *hahs* and the whip of fabric slicing through the air. The unmistakable intonation of a man taunting another man. My dad watched everything at top volume. The rest of us learned to sleep through all the fighting.

Sometimes Anh and I would tag along to Saigon Market because we knew we could have dried squid and sesame candy while my dad talked and joked with his friends. We would go outside to divide the treats, careful not to lean against the exhaust-stained siding that the store shared with the Waterbed Gallery next door. We couldn't help but watch all the cars speeding past us, four lanes in two different directions.

———

When I found the photograph of my mother that summer day when I was briefly home from college, I was looking for the childhood books that I had gotten to choose, for free, during the Reading Is Fundamental book fairs in elementary school. Though I still had my well-worn copy of *Harriet the Spy*, I had lost *The Girl with the Silver Eyes*, *The Pinballs*, *The Hundred Dresses*, and *Wild Violets*, and I feared that my dad and stepmom had thrown them out. They'd always said I read too much, and no one in my family seemed to think books were something worth keeping anyway; that's why there were libraries. I was alone in the house, having woken up late and verified that my dad and stepmom's cars were gone from the driveway. All these years, they'd had their own lives and I hadn't bothered to pay attention. Where were they? Why was I even visiting during the summer, when I had a cheap sublet? Even my grandmother Noi had moved on. Her former bedroom had become a place for storage, for all the purchases and products that my parents were so certain they would get to, someday.

Instead of the books I found appliance manuals and dried-out pens rubber-banded together; I found boxes filled with dot-matrix printer paper, clothes from department stores that no longer existed. And then, in a plastic tub of insurance forms and piles of negatives from those days when we had to wait for pictures to be developed, I found what I had never searched for—my mother, in a black-and-white photograph, back when she was young. She's standing near an open window of a stone house. Her satin flowered dress has three-quarter sleeves and a flaring skirt. Her hair is pulled into a near-beehive updo. I don't know if I've been born yet. How this picture came to be, and to be here, I would never know. Maybe my dad took the picture and kept it all that time, crossing the world between Vietnam and Michigan, and all those years in which no one ever spoke of my mother.

Of course, we were all scared of my dad. His temper used to be sudden and ferocious; it could make all the light in the house go out. After, I could never remember what set him off. But I could tell you about plates of food thrown against the wall. The sound of a glass being shattered on purpose.

Because we didn't talk about the war in Vietnam we also didn't talk about trauma. We didn't talk about violence either. We just watched it, all the time, in movies.

Of course, my dad spanked my sister and me. It's a generational thing, we say now, trying to explain this to our own kids, who have never been spanked. Kids used to get spankings all the time and this was considered normal, even at school, where the principal had the right to "paddle" a kid as punishment.

My older son asked me to describe it, once. He was about eight years old and he wanted to know: What was spanking, exactly? What actually happened? So I told him what my dad would do. It wasn't often, I said, though I never recalled what we were being spanked for. But my sister and I would have to lie on our stomachs, side by side on a bed. My dad would take a stick—

What kind of stick? my son asked, but I didn't remember.

A yardstick? Well, he always had extra lumber in the garage, from his various home projects. And then he'd hit us across our thighs a few times.

That must have hurt so much, my son said, and I remembered that my sister and I would scream from the shock as much as from the pain. I'm sorry that happened to you, my son said.

I hardly knew how to respond. Maybe that's an American thing, apologizing for someone else's pain in which you've had no part, and I've never gotten used to it. The Vietnamese phrase for "I'm sorry," "Xin loi," was something I learned in a Vietnamese-language class I took in college. I never heard it, growing up, and never expected to.

"I'm sorry" is also what people tend to say when I tell them the story of my mother, that is, when I have to, when I find myself unable to avoid answering questions about her. She has become, after all, a story more than a mother. One reason I never questioned my dad about her is because I was scared of his anger and scared of the shame involved in making him feel or remember something. I didn't think he would punish me if I asked, but I knew we would both keep the wound of my asking, forever. So I didn't. I didn't snoop. Didn't go looking through his room. For all of my childhood, it was easier not to seek and not to find. It all created a sense of absence, yes—a kind of secret, a silence—but I learned that a person can live with this. It becomes part of you, so much that you almost forget that it wasn't supposed to be there at all.

———

I was in middle school when my dad acquired a VCR. He would go to the video store every week, heading straight to the Action/Adventure section, where he would get three or four movies, and watch them over and over, never caring how late it got. The rest of us learned to live with it. My dad began a quest to get a larger, fancier television, with larger, fancier speakers, as much as he could possibly afford. He longed for surround sound. He started to buy the movies outright, so he could watch them again anytime. The VHS tapes gathered by the TV set, later joined by DVDs, then Blu-rays. He wanted to keep the images, play them at his command: hand-to-hand combat, guys battling evil forces, men against aliens, against disaster, against the world. Even the musical scores were ominous and militaristic. My dad, who had fought in what is called the Vietnam War, who was made a refugee by that war, has rented and watched the same racist Vietnam War movies that many Americans take as truth: *Platoon*; *Good Morning, Vietnam*; *Full Metal Jacket*. I don't know how he can stand it, how he can watch depictions of Vietnamese men being killed over and over, and see white men joke about it. But I never asked him this question because in our household we did not talk about the war. We only listened to the made-up sounds of battle and death and dying.

———

Every time I have seen my mother, she has told me how she discovered we had left for America. By now, I can't distinguish what she said at which visit. The house was empty, is what she always says. No one there.

They all left for America, a neighbor told her.

No note! she says. No nothing.

Every time, I have asked the same question in return: What did you do?

What did I do? I went home. I cried and cried.

———

Childhood felt slow when I was in it, until suddenly I wasn't. My sisters left for college and I couldn't wait to leave, too. I didn't hate high school—I was lucky because nothing too horrible happened to me, and I had some good friends, some good English teachers, even a boyfriend. But it was all a waiting room. A long act of endurance with a soundtrack of shoes squeaking on the gym floor, lockers slamming shut. And I never stopped hating the cottage-like house whose windows refused to let in enough light. I guessed that my stepmom thought moving there would fix the arguments—about money, about my dad's late nights—and it did, eventually, but not until everyone else had gone.

My siblings and I would never live at home again. My uncles would move to their own apartments, start their own families. Foster brothers would live with us for a while and then leave. Noi, too, would go live with one of my uncles to help raise his son.

I was so busy wanting to be somewhere and someone else that I almost never thought about my mother. We had moved houses—would she even know how to find us? How had she known where we were, in the first place? When such questions popped into my mind—and it was seldom that they did—I knew how to push them back.

Then I was off to the University of Michigan, which I could afford with Pell grants, work-study, and some federal loans. I lived with a roommate in a dorm, then with more roommates in an apartment. Suddenly I had so many hours all to myself, studying in hushed reading rooms where tables had green-shaded lighting fixtures that I later learned were called bankers lamps. I memorized poems, like Elizabeth Bishop's "One Art," because the art of losing wasn't hard to master. I walked countless miles around campus and combed for books in the stacks of the libraries, always going back to write in what was called the Fishbowl of Angell Hall, a gigantic sunken space filled with computers and printers that students had to sign up to use. I had no one to answer to but myself. Once, after an evening astronomy class, I sat down on the winter-cold stone steps of the building and cried with what I realized was happiness.

I rarely communicated with my parents during college. The university had a basic form of email called Pine, but it would be years before everyone had modems and AOL. I never called just to talk—what was there to say? They didn't call me either. Before cell phones, long-distance calls cost ten cents or more a minute, depending on the time of day. I would go weeks, sometimes months, without speaking to my dad or stepmom or anyone in my family. We only talked when we had to figure out holidays and what time I'd be arriving at their house—home, we all said, though it had never felt that way to me.

There I would find my dad watching the same action movies that I had always refused to watch. I was an English major and wanted to see movies that my new friends and professors referenced. My dad derided them as boring, too much talking. I once rented *Paper Moon* and my dad grumbled, It's in black and white, too?! before falling asleep on the sofa. Did I think I was somehow better because I liked *Paper Moon* more than car chase movies? Did I think all those *Missions Impossible* and *Terminators* were lowbrow, a term I had learned in college? Yes, I did. I was convinced that action movies were bad and talk-heavy movies were good and I had so much catching up to do. My classmates had already clocked years watching the good movies, the ones that were called independent films. Every new thing I learned was tinged with the embarrassment of not having known it before.

A few years ago, I watched *Paper Moon* again. It's about a messy, messed-up, yet endearing father-daughter relationship, set during the Depression. I rooted for that con artist dad and for the daughter who becomes a con artist, too. The threat of violence—what happens if you're caught, what happens if you're found out, if you fail, if you run out of money, or gas, or time—is in the background, and it keeps the characters moving. *Paper Moon*, I realized, was one long, talk-heavy, black-and-white chase movie.

In Boston, my mother sometimes had Vietnamese melodramas playing on the television when I visited. I liked this, because it was useful to have something else to focus on in the room. Everywhere you go in America, if you're Vietnamese, you can find a grocery with *Paris by Night* videos to rent and buy. I still associate my mother with these images, though the last two times I visited her in Boston she had no TV at all.

It was during my second visit to Boston, after college, that I asked her about the photograph. I described the girl in the picture, the dress, the hair. Did she remember it?

No idea, she said. But do I look pretty?

I asked how she and my dad had met. Such a story, she said. Why would you want to know that?

———

At some point, after I found the photograph of my mother, I watched an action movie with my dad. It was winter break and there was nothing else to do but sit down on the old L-shaped sofa and face *Die Hard 3: With a Vengeance*, starring Bruce Willis. My dad was a fan of this franchise, and this installment featured Samuel L. Jackson as a reluctant accomplice and Jeremy Irons as the bad guy. The story line involves Jeremy Irons setting up riddles for the heroes to solve, which somehow connects to his goals of avenging his brother and stealing gold bricks from the Federal Reserve. Of course, the good guys prevail. They dodge hundreds of bullets and survive massive explosions.

I found myself curious, then interested, then riveted. I laughed with my dad when the guys drove wildly through Central Park. Whenever I said wow or oh no, or covered my eyes, my dad was delighted. Good movie, he said when the credits began. He'd seen it before but still seemed to feel the satisfaction of time well spent. I couldn't disagree.

Over the next years, whenever I visited my parents, I watched more action movies with my dad. We watched

Speed, The Fugitive, Clear and Present Danger, Broken Arrow, Independence Day, Con Air, Face/Off, Dante's Peak, Armageddon, Deep Impact, Enemy of the State, The Bourne Identity, Minority Report (which, to my disappointment, was not about the political status of minorities in the United States). During the movies, we didn't talk about anything but what was happening on the screen. My dad would admire the choreography of a fight scene, a perfect leap. I was the one always bracing for bloodshed. I would close my eyes and look away. My dad never looked away; he looked closer. Sometimes he would rewind to see an action sequence again.

You never get nightmares from watching these movies? I asked him once, and he said, No, never. The good movies just make it look as real as possible. Real life, you know, is not this. I had spent much of my childhood tensing up whenever he walked into the room, gauging his mood; I had spent my childhood searching for a way out. I had never thought about how maybe he wanted a way out, too.

———

My dad is one of four brothers. In Vietnam, during the war, he was a tank gunner. One of his brothers was in the air force, another in the navy. His oldest brother was also in the army. I know him only as the uncle who died in the war, whose photo has always sat on the altar that my grandmother Noi kept and that my dad and stepmom now keep.

My dad and my uncles do not talk about the war in terms of combat. They almost never talk about it at all. The war is a reference point; it is the reason we are here in the United States.

My mother does not talk about the war either. Whenever I have asked her what life was like in Vietnam, back then, she has laughed, letting me know that the question was ridiculous, too big. Of course, she had come of age during wartime. I tried to imagine her meeting my dad and hanging out at a party. I imagined them laughing through a haze of cigarette smoke. I could see my dad—the best ballroom dancer I know, the kind of dancer people turn to watch—holding out his hand. Maybe they had secret meetup spots; maybe they went to parties and only talked to each other. Maybe one day my dad borrowed his best friend's camera and took a picture.

———

Once, when I was in eighth grade, I tried to skip school because my parents refused to let me join a field trip. It might have been the cost, or the fact that it was a full day away. But I was embarrassed, and pretended to be sick so I wouldn't have to be one of the few losers at school whose parents had said no. My dad knew I was faking, though, and told me I'd better not miss the school bus. We were alone: my sisters had already left for their high school classes; my younger brother was already at his elementary school; my stepmom was already at work. My grandmother—I don't remember where she was. She, who would not kill a bug or spider but gently set them outside, was the only one who could keep my dad's temper from escalating, when the rest of us just got out of his way. But even she could not stop him entirely.

There were pieces of plywood stacked all over the house for my dad's ongoing and abandoned renovation projects. He picked up one of these pieces and struck my leg. Go to school, he yelled. It all happened so fast. I was wearing the same clothes I'd worn the day before because that's what I'd lazily changed into when I woke up. There was no time to do anything else but put on my shoes. My dad held the stick in the air—the brandishing, threatening position I knew from so many movies. I ran out of the house. He came after me, stick in hand, shouting, to make sure that I didn't miss the bus on purpose. He chased me up the driveway, which was nearly a quarter mile long, part of that ideal of living out in the country that he and my stepmom had said they wanted. It sounded almost fancy, a long driveway, and at school I pretended it was.

I saw the bus approaching. The driver was kind; whenever she saw me rushing to the stop, she would wait. I saw other kids on the bus stare out the windows, not at me but at my dad, who stood maybe thirty feet from me, still holding the stick. I got on the bus and sat down. I didn't have my school-bag or any of my books. If anyone spoke to me, I have blocked that out. The day was mercifully quiet, almost everyone else away on the field trip. The hours went by in a fog and then I was back on the bus, headed home. I knew my dad's anger would have long subsided by then, and he wasn't there any-way. It was over: we would never speak of that morning, and he would never strike me again. In my grandmother's room, which was filled with plants she tended every day, I watched the last half hour of *Santa Barbara* and ate the sliced fruit she gave me and worked on one of her thousand-piece jig-saw puzzles. It was satisfying to select a piece at random and find that it fit, that it made the broken scenery a little clearer. Sometimes now, when I feel my own temper flaring, when my kids are getting on my last nerve, as my stepmom would have said, my mind takes me back to Noi's room with its blue carpet. I do not mean that she was the peaceful antidote. Just that she allowed space. For thinking, for contemplating what to do with anger, its deep and many sources.

A couple of years later, in high school, a girl I will call Tanya turned to me in Spanish class and said, You can laugh about yourself, right? We were doing group work, and the others looked up, interested. Tanya said she was reminded of something she saw in eighth grade, on the school bus. We were at your stop, she said, and your dad came running after you with a stick. She laughed and the others in our group joined in. What was that about? Tanya asked. She was a girl everyone would have called sweet. We had been friends in middle school, and though we'd drifted apart, weren't on bad terms. I answered the only way I knew how: I laughed, too. I said I didn't know, that it was just some dumb thing, that my dad was always doing dumb stuff. El valiente o el borracho? I said exaggeratedly, referring to two cards in the bingo game that our teacher often had us play. Everyone loved the image of el borracho, a man with a bottle in one hand, mid-stagger, and just saying it shifted the talk elsewhere, as I knew it would. I was getting better at things like that. I was learning how to cover for myself.

—

I have watched the *Bourne Identity* movies dozens of times. I've seen them with my dad and I've seen them on my own. On purpose, as background, as something to keep me company while cooking. I can't watch horror movies without having nightmares, but if I see an action movie enough, if I see disaster enough, I start to return to them as a strange form of comfort. Like *Paper Moon*, the Bourne movies are extended chase scenes. The thrill is in watching the protagonist learn what he's capable of, watching him outsmart everyone else. But Jason Bourne doesn't really triumph. He's only alive because he has killed so many others. He's alive because someone killed his girlfriend instead of him. He's alive because women keep helping him. Like so many heroes, Jason Bourne is essentially alone. He must live with who he is and was. We, the audience, are asked to forgive, to feel sorry for, a former assassin; the redemption he gets is through us.

Action movies always show minor characters making the wrong decisions. The people who think they can outrun a storm. The people who decide to stand on rooftops and wave hello to alien spaceships. The hero, though—the hero always makes the right decisions. The hero knows when to stay and when to leave. Sometimes, watching these movies, I wonder: Would I know what to do in such situations? Would I make the right call? And I think no, I probably wouldn't. I wouldn't greet alien spaceships, but maybe I would try to walk through a storm. Probably I would take the wrong path, try to cross the wrong two wires. I have no idea how to survive.

After so many years, after all these action movies, I have learned that I, too, have a relationship with violence and war—it's just that I don't understand it. I'm an American who is here because of war, yet I retain no actual memory of war or of becoming a refugee. It's in me through proximity, through absorption, through inheritance. It is the self that's taken my whole life to get nearer to, in order to perceive: once a refugee, always a refugee, no matter how well hidden it is.

Does my dad see his life in terms of an action movie, with war and violence and suspense? He made it to the other side—America, survival—in literal and figurative ways. He settled in a place where he can watch movies all night, by himself, in a home that's tucked away so that no one from the street could ever know what he's doing. His identity is secret to me, always will be. He carries with him a thousand untold stories.

By the time I found that photo of my mother, I didn't even, at that point, think of any of his actions as violent, though that may sound strange. They were just vague echoes of something that began in violence—a historical body of violence; a systemic violence. I do not mean this as an excuse. I mean that I am trying to understand.

In America, we grow up with the word *hero* as something good and powerful. But anyone who studies literature knows that heroes are complicated figures who often create their own suffering and tragedy. The hero makes decisions that seem right or necessary but then has to contend with the consequences. For my dad, who may or may not think of himself as the hero of his own story, those consequences are immeasurable loss: a brother, a country; possibly, my mother. Every day in the United States is a kind of loss when you know that starting over is on someone else's terms.

———

My dad today is not the dad I grew up with, and hasn't been for many years. The shift started after I went to college. Every time I came home he would say, Are you hungry? Do you want to eat? Do you want McDonald's? Burger King? He would get me a bulk box of my favorite instant ramen. When he learned how to cook, he would make meal packets, like shrimp in a homemade soy-ginger-garlic sauce, that I could take back to my apartment and freeze. All you have to do is make rice, he'd say. He planned enormous feasts for holidays, built a bar in the corner of the party room, installed a professional-looking karaoke system.

And he is so gentle with my children. When we visit, he heaps them with praise that I never heard as a kid, how they're such good kids, such bright kids. He is always offering them food, a new toy, or outright cash. I figure, it's the kind of thing Vietnamese grandparents do. Once, during a holiday, I searched something kid related on my phone, to find an answer, and my dad suddenly said, I wish we had Google when you guys were little. I didn't know how to respond. He said, There's so much we didn't know back then.

I have studied my children's sleeping patterns. I have consulted parenting books. But I am still so often wrong about what my kids need. Maybe they weren't tired, but just hungry. Maybe they needed to go for a walk. Maybe they wanted to be soothed; maybe they didn't want to be soothed at all. I am trial-and-erroring all the time. I am never really prepared, only anxious. Parenting, I know now, is a long relationship with failure.

Sometimes, I want to call my dad and tell him I am okay, ask if he is okay. I am not looking for an apology. I am not looking for xin loi. I have no need for it. Maybe I just want to know what happened, to fill in the blanks: like that old motorboat we never used and that just stayed in the driveway—when did that disappear? What happened to all those broken-down cars? Who took that photo of my mother? Was it you? What happened in the moments before, and in the moments after? Maybe I also want the impossible: to have the answers without asking the questions. To reconcile the past as if it weren't still with me.

In a way, I am still afraid of my dad. Not of his temper, which has long since faded with age. I am afraid of hurting him. In my mind, the look on his face stops me. It's a guardedness, a troubled frown, cast down, probably like the one I have, too, redolent with that old refugee shame, the one that was imposed on us before we ever knew it. I am afraid of hurting him even though I know it's too late.

———

It's late at night in the 1990s. My siblings are in different cities; my stepmom has fallen asleep; my mother is riding a bus through Boston. My children are years from being born. My dad and I watch television, the volume so loud there is no place in the house free of gunfire and grenades. He is still on a quest to get as big of a television as he can afford. A 40-inch screen is, in his opinion, paltry. It's settling. Still we settle, down onto the old puffy leather sofas, to watch the action movies he loves. The living room fills with images of machine guns waving and spraying. Knives slashing. Fists hitting their mark. Cars smash onto sidewalks, fly in slow-motion arcs through the air.

My dad will fall asleep to these scenes, unwilling to let the movie end or the television rest. Let's see it again, he'll say the next day, reaching for the remote control. I want to know how to pull back the days that have slipped from our grasp. I want to talk to my dad, explain that I had to find that photograph in order to find *her*, to allow the portrait of her past into my present life. But he and I don't speak in such ways, at least not yet. In his favorite movies, there is little dialogue and the heroes have perfect balance. They fling themselves from building to building as if they already know they're safe, that the resolution, the soft shore of the fade to black, is already waiting to welcome them into that beckoning landscape where all the avenues point forward.

5

APPARENT, PART II

After I graduated from college, I taught in a summer scholars program at a boarding school outside of Boston. It was a two-month fellowship I had applied for back in the winter, when I was casting around for funding. I couldn't afford to backpack around Europe, but I could buy a plane ticket to Boston, and I would get free dorm housing and cafeteria food. I had also decided this would be a chance to be near my mother, a chance to get to know her. I would spend a few days with her and her family after the fellowship ended, but maybe I would also meet her for tea or dinner in the city, each of us taking buses or trains from different directions.

At the boarding school, I was assigned a dorm in one of the white clapboard colonial-style buildings that arced around the main campus. I was supposed to look after a small group of high school girls who would be living in that same dorm, help teach an English lit class, and assist an extra-curricular aerobics class. I had never, outside of my own PE classes in high school, engaged in aerobics and was generally hopeless at sports. But all teaching fellows had to help with some activity and aerobics was the one that required the least amount of knowledge.

As a thoroughly midwestern public school kid, I couldn't walk the campus of the school without thinking about the mysteries of wealth, of East Coast manners and white, moneyed lives. *Gatsby* and *The Age of Innocence* had given me glimpses, but not knowledge, exactly. I, more accustomed to strip malls, which had not yet achieved wider cultural appreciation in the form of irony, felt like a trespasser on the campus. The boarding school had a grand bell tower, an obelisk that, I was told, seniors would climb up and rappel down as part of some tradition. The administration building had big, wide steps, like at a liberal arts college, and a lapis lazuli clock. I looked at that clock every chance I could get, as if to memorize its intensity of blue. I hadn't given much thought to this summer plan. Back in the winter, it had seemed straightforward: do the fellowship, spend a few days with my mother and her family. But the campus had a way of making me feel removed from the world—which I guessed was the point—as if prior intentions no longer mattered.

At the fellowship orientation I fell into instant friendship with two other women. It's a thing that had happened to me once or twice before but seldom since: the lightning bolt of friendship, as intoxicating as falling in love but maybe better. Jodi and Lily and I were immediately inseparable. We sat in the dining hall together, laughed through meetings, hung out in each other's dorm room. The teaching we had come to do became tangential to the pursuit of friendship. On weekday mornings, classes paused for literal cookies and milk, set out on tables on the main lawn, another of the school's many old traditions. Jodi and Lily and I would stand together, the three of us with our backs to the rest of the world. I was teaching literature, Jodi was teaching advanced algebra, and Lily was teaching biology, and Jodi, too, had been assigned to the aerobics class. We laughed about this every day. At night we would roam the nearby town, get pizza, try to convince one of us to buy things like a slutty backless tank top made out of a handkerchief. We went to a karaoke bar, gave fake names, and sang "Sweet Dreams." We never stopped talking and I had never laughed so much. It felt like we had our whole lives to catch up on and only this summer to do it.

I might have gone on like this, nearly forgetting my

mother an hour away in Boston, if she hadn't called the phone in my dorm room one Saturday morning, a couple of weeks into the summer, waking me up. She had gotten the number from my dad, who was and always would be our go-between. I had never spoken to my mother on the phone before and suddenly there she was, her voice loud, as if already in mid-speech, with a hello that sounded vaguely accusatory, distrusting of telephonic communication. Hello, she called out. Where are you? When are you going to visit me?

I felt annoyed, which then made me feel ashamed, like my teenage self sulking about visiting relatives instead of getting to hang out with friends. But I was also taken aback by her insistence. I hardly knew this woman, and here she was acting like a parent, demanding that I visit? By that point, so caught up with Jodi and Lily, I had almost forgotten that I had planned to see her at all. The visits I had imagined seemed ridiculous now, even juvenile. A fantasy. We had only met that one time, a few summers before. We didn't know each other at all, really. What would we even talk about?

So I said I wasn't sure. I didn't have a car, and the school was at least an hour away, longer by bus and train.

We will bring you a car, my mother said.

Even now, I can see the configuration of that dorm room: the little bed pushed against a wall; the nearby desk facing the window. I can see myself sitting up in that bed, reading. Weeks later, I would bring a boy there and never tell anyone. The room received a startling amount of light, emphasizing how empty, how spare, it was. How large it seemed then, though I'm sure it wasn't. My clothes were still in my suitcase and would be kept there, even after wearing and washing. I was not then, nor am I now, really, a person who puts away and hangs up all her clothes. I am not a person who moves into a new space that easily.

I tried to tell my mother that I didn't need a car. She told me that her daughter's husband had an extra one and they would bring it tomorrow. When I protested, she protested, her voice growing louder. She demanded the name and address of the school. She said they would be there the next afternoon.

———

They showed up in two cars: my brother-in-law driving his tan-colored van, my half sister driving that Plymouth Sundance, her kids in the back and our mother in the front.

My memory does not retain the details of this day in the parking lot near the dormitory building. Had I known to expect them at a certain time? Had they rung the doorbell of the dorm? I keep, instead, that Sunday feeling of drowsiness. The campus was so quiet and I wondered where everyone was. I keep that moment when I understood that my mother and her family had no intention of lingering. This was not, after all, a visit. It was already afternoon and they had plenty to do before the workweek began. The kids, my niece and nephew, tumbled out of the car and into the van. They had all driven here to hand over this Plymouth and now they were going to leave.

My half sister held out the keys. She smiled, gave a quick hug, said a compliment about what I was wearing. I wanted to ask her why everyone was being so nice to me. My mother said, Be good and be careful. I promised that I would be very careful with the car. She rolled her eyes—she wasn't talking about the car.

She got into the front seat of the van, next to her son-in-law, and my half sister got in the back with the kids. They waved, all of them waving and smiling, as they drove out of that parking lot. The whole thing had taken less than fifteen minutes.

For a while, I stood there by myself and regarded that Plymouth Sundance. It was the same maroon-burgundy color inside and out. It was a kind of car that doesn't even exist anymore. Compact, utilitarian, the stuff of bargain rentals. I had no need for it, and nowhere I wanted to go.

The summer began to blur. I woke early, helped teach literature classes that I no longer remember, had cookies and milk, had lunch, had dinner, tried to do my own writing. The students were smart and well behaved, or maybe I mean well trained. They participated in class; they did not turn in papers late. They had come from all over the country and world for this summer program and I figured they also came from money or enough money, since that was the kind of school it was. They knew just what was expected of them.

Several times I showed up for aerobics. Jodi, because she'd once taken such classes, became the lead teacher. I followed along with the students. We were a small group—everyone else preferred activities like tennis—and we did our thing in a dance studio, with mirrors all around. The supply closet had a collection of CDs with energetic music that Jodi played in the background while demonstrating moves. She would shout out the changes: Now do the grapevine! That's the one I could do because it was easy footwork and when I looked in the mirror it looked like a synchronized, ridiculous dance. Lily started showing up, too, just for fun, and the three of us would get through the forty-five minutes trying not to laugh. We spent a lot of time on stretching and warming up and cooling down. After, we'd go to our dorms and change, then meet up again. Other fellows would join us at dinner, but mostly we remained a separate unit, the three of us finding something in each other that we'd held back from others, possibly our whole lives. I had never before talked to friends about my mother; the subject was too complicated, too vulnerable. I feared that people would look at me differently, pityingly. But it was different with Jodi and Lily, maybe because it was a summer of what felt like suspended time, or maybe because they both talked freely about their own complicated family situations, defined by silence and struggle, financial worries, late-night fights. When I explained about my mother, and the car they had brought, Jodi and Lily seemed to get it right away. Our families are fucked up, Jodi said. It was such a relief to hear it. We were not rich kids, but here we were, with all of our hidden family messes, teaching them.

About a week after my Boston family dropped off the Plymouth Sundance, Lily said we should drive somewhere. It was a weekday afternoon, just the two of us because Jodi had to proctor a biology test. We had no plan in mind when we got into the car. Lily, who had spent part of her childhood in Boston, said that the drivers of Massachusetts were crazy. I was not a confident driver and kept to the residential neighborhoods around the school.

We were only a few minutes from campus when I realized the brakes weren't working. I said this out loud to Lily, who didn't even panic. Just keep trying it, she said. I did. I pressed the brake harder, but the car kept moving. We were going all of 25 miles an hour, but we weren't stopping. No one else was on the road, but up ahead we could see that it sloped downhill.

Somehow Lily and I were both calm. She advised me to put the car into neutral. It didn't help. I was pretty sure this scenario had not been covered in driver's ed, and we were getting too close to the hill. So all at once I pushed down the parking brake as hard as I could. The car made a dreadful grinding sound and shuddered to a stop. I threw the gear into park and Lily and I jumped out, as if the whole car were going to blow up. It didn't. The street remained still, lined with quiet houses and trees. (Where was everyone? Did they all go to beach houses in the summer?) Lily and I burst into laughter. What were we going to do? Neither of us had AAA and a tow service would be too expensive. In the end, we decided just to try the car again. Maybe, we said, it was like restarting a computer; maybe the brakes would be okay now.

And they were. I turned the car around, away from the hill, and drove slowly back to the school and to the parking spot where my mother's family had dropped off the car. Lily and I jumped out again, laughing again. That thing, she said, is a Deathmobile. When we told the story to Jodi, later, the word stuck. That's what we called it for the next couple of weeks until I tried the car again—why, I can't remember—and realized that the Deathmobile had become the Deadmobile.

Not long after this, my mother left a message on my dorm phone's voice mail. She said she had called and called, but I never answered. When I called her back, she said, Where are you? I said, What do you mean? I'm here where you called me. But she meant, *Why are you not* here? She meant why had I not visited yet. But I had a good excuse: the Deadmobile.

She made a clicking, sighing noise that I recognized as deeply Vietnamese, something I'd heard my dad and uncles and grandmother do. Never mind, she said. She said her son-in-law would fix it.

When they'd first dropped off that car, I kept asking if they were sure. Didn't they need it for themselves? They had waved that question away. It had taken me more than half the summer to understand what should have been so clear: they had dropped off the car so I could drive it to visit them in Boston. I had never even tried.

———

Instead, one Saturday morning Jodi and Lily and I took a train to New York because I had never been there before. When I was growing up in Michigan, everyone referred to Chicago as the big city. New York might as well have been a different country. I have no idea where Jodi and Lily took me—some restaurant, some bar, so many crowds. Just knowing we were in New York, even if for less than thirty-six hours, felt like a private joy to keep in my midwestern heart. It was a thrill to hear the subway as it approached, to participate in the casual way everyone stood there waiting. I wanted to ask them, how did people get to stay here? How did they manage to make this their everyday life? That night we stayed with friends of Jodi's who lived in Murray Hill, in what looked like an office building off Lexington Avenue. We slept on the floor of a tiny living room, and it seemed amazing that no one seemed to mind—not the people who lived in that apartment, not me or Jodi or Lily. I figured, this was what it was like to live here. You shared the space you had.

You have to understand: I had never gone on a spring break excursion, didn't have family vacations outside of a stressful trip to Disney World when I was ten and Niagara Falls a couple years after that. That summer with Jodi and Lily was the closest I'd ever been to something that felt like a holiday. The only thing that kept me in check was my constant worry about money. I was living off the modest fellowship and meager savings. I had to be careful, and think ahead to fall expenses. I knew the shame of a balance too low to withdraw money from at the ATM.

I fell asleep on the train returning us to Boston. By the

time we got back to the dorms, it was late Sunday night. Slipping past the parking lot to let myself into my dorm building, I saw the Deadmobile in its same spot. It embarrassed me. The boxy shape of it, the very existence of it, the way it reminded me of driver's ed. The deadness of it. I never wanted to be in that car again.

On the students' last morning, parents arrived in time for cookies and milk and an early lunch reception on the broad lawn. I had gotten to know my students enough over the two months to feel a tender worrying about their future choices and future selves, and so it was strange to say such a final good-bye. We were not friends, and social media didn't exist yet; we would never see or recognize each other again.

It would be the same with most of my fellow fellows. Our long good-bye had started the night before, with a fancy meal in the dining hall. Fancy meaning tablecloths were used, and china plates printed with the school's name and insignia in a deep, lapis lazuli blue. I stole one of those plates. Tucked it in my bag and carried it away, and later packed it in my suitcase. I still have the plate, somewhere in storage, never used.

After the students left, the whole campus seemed to take on a stilled, empty feeling, and I went back to my dorm to finish packing before the fellows' last dinner and party. It was also my last night in this room, this building, and I left the door open to the silent hall, the windows open to the afternoon. The air was brilliant—the soft yellow light of a perfect summer day, the kind that makes you feel joy whether you mean to or not, the kind that also makes you recognize the distant certainty of fall. Instead of packing my suitcase I sat down at my desk and started writing. I have no idea what I was writing then. A story or a poem or scattered thoughts on the page. Odd to think of all those typed words, perhaps as earnest as the ones I'm typing now. Getting made, getting saved. And one day disappearing, or turning into something else that also disappears.

I wrote until it was time to meet Lily downstairs. Her dorm was the farthest from the dining hall and we'd fallen into a pattern of her stopping by my building and then the two of us stopping by Jodi's. Standing outside, I realized that the parking lot was empty. The Deadmobile wasn't there. Had my half sister's husband come here on his own, jump-started the car, and driven away, just like that? How long had the car been gone?

The fellows' farewell dinner was takeout food in a meeting room with the lights turned down and hip-hop music in the background. Everyone was talking about what was next, even though we'd all talked about it before. Jodi and Lily and I, like a lot of the other fellows, were going to graduate programs in different fields, in different states.

At some point, Ben came over to talk to us. Ben was the best-looking male fellow in the whole group. For weeks, we had all flirted with him in the mild, uncommitted way I had learned to do in college, as practice and a way to pass the time. He was not the guy I'd had that one night with. He was too good-looking; I would've had to tell Jodi and Lily about it, and I had no interest in a summer fling. I was too busy with a summer friendship.

At the party, Ben said he liked my dress, which was Lily's. She had made me borrow it because she said it would suit me. Simple black silk crepe, bias-cut, a square neck that rounded into thin straps, very later nineties. It was sexy, Ben said, and I laughed at the word, how he said it the way I imagined a middle-aged guy would say it. Someone passed around vodka and tequila that other fellows had brought. After a while, we all flowed out onto the wide lawns of the main campus.

I do not know who started the idea—it very well could have been me—but I can tell you exactly what happened next: Jodi, Lily, and I took Ben to an empty dorm room. It had been stripped and cleaned, or perhaps had never been used that summer. We kept the lights off, but I can still see the stolid old desk and chair, the shelves, and the bed that someone had pushed against the window. We had lured Ben with a promise of a four-way. Let's trick him, one of us said. It's not that we had anything against him. He had not wronged us and he was not a bad guy. He was merely good-looking, and he was right in front of us, and we'd had a summer of feeling powerful and we wanted our last night to feel even more powerful.

We had accomplished this so quickly, getting Ben in that room, that we hadn't thought to figure out what would happen next. Ben sat down on the bare mattress and looked at us. Jodi, Lily, and I looked at each other.

Lie down, I said to Ben. He did.

I glanced at my friends, but they were looking at me like, What now? I think we were all thinking the same thing, which was, Are we actually doing this?

Ben was wearing a plaid shirt, jeans, a belt. I have no idea what he studied or taught, what his plans were, what his last name was. Enough light came in from the streetlamps around campus, enough for me to see him, to remember him, lying on that mattress in that dorm room. He would have stayed as long as we told him to.

I bent down and unbuckled his belt with my teeth.

If I had been alone with Ben, I might have continued. But the performance wasn't for him; it was for my friends. I looked up. They were impressed, maybe even a little in awe. And that was what I had wanted.

And then we began to laugh. We grabbed each other and fled the room, the dorm building. We ran across campus, leaving Ben on that bed with his belt undone.

We made our way to one of the enormous majestic old oak trees on the lawn and collapsed there, lying back to gauge the full canopy of leaves above us. It was glorious. They—the leaves, the women—were glorious. Is it too much if I admit this was one of the most joyful moments I have known in my life? I was in my early twenties. I had, just a few months before, graduated from college. I understood that I was young in a way I would never feel again, and I wanted to know if *this* was what it was supposed to be like. I wanted to keep my eyes open just to keep that moment, that night, that canopy, that laughter.

———

In the morning it felt like I was the last person left on campus, waiting outside the dorm for my mother's family to pick me up, as we had planned, so I could stay with them for a few days. They arrived in the resurrected Deadmobile. My half sister said that her husband and one of his friends had driven out to the school the week before and jump-started the car. They hadn't found any problems with the brakes. I sat in the back seat, rolled down the window. I closed my eyes and felt the heat of the day gather in the same way it had when I was a kid, sitting in the back seat of my stepmom's cars—the secondhand Oldsmobile Cutlass Supreme, the Ford Tempo—waiting for her to finish running errands. It felt like there was nothing to look forward to. The exhilaration of the night before seemed long gone; the two months with Jodi and Lily fell away and I was my small self again. No one powerful. Just another person stuck in circumstances made long before.

If I felt like a child, it was because I had never learned how to talk to my family—any idea of family. I was stuck in the silences, the fear of asking simple questions. I once told a boyfriend that people in my family didn't say "I love you." We didn't kiss; we didn't hug; we didn't ask how everyone was doing. The boyfriend, white, had been shocked. He called it borderline abusive, which made me regret saying anything at all. I couldn't explain, even to myself, the feeling of how silence replicates itself: the less you say, the less you feel allowed to say.

I did know some forms of love: My grandmother Noi slicing up fruit every single day for my siblings and me, icing pineapple and canned lychees in the summer. My dad checking on my sisters' cars, my dad making sure I had those boxes of my favorite instant ramen. My stepmom dropping me off at the library and, once in a great while, stopping for cheeseburgers on the way home. And my new family in

Boston bringing me a Plymouth Sundance, an hour away from where they lived, in case I needed it.

In truth, I didn't know what to do with this kind of love. I didn't know how to return it. Even that word, *return*, never sounded right to me. It sounded like giving it back, like getting a refund at a store.

In the sprawl of squat buildings within the complex where my Boston family lived, my half sister and her husband had a two-bedroom apartment one building over from my mother's one-bedroom. The plan was for me to stay a few days in the bigger place, where I could borrow one of the kids' beds while they bunked together.

I have been trying to keep my niece and nephew out of this story. They were so little then, barely elementary school age, and they looked at me without history or expectation, which would never happen again. I was in awe at how seamlessly they switched between English and Vietnamese. I watched them laugh with my mother, their ba ngoai, maternal grandmother. She teased and scolded, brought them candies and told them to share, almost like the way my own grandmother Noi did with my sister and me, parceling out treats so that we would feel equally favored.

I can't remember much of those brief days with my Boston family. Far from being emotional or intense, they were filled with quiet. I hardly saw my mother at all.

She was working; she had to go out. Many years later, I would recognize this as the vague language of parenting. I felt then, as maybe everyone else did, too, uncertain. I didn't know how to behave, what to do, what to say.

One day I walked with my mother to the factory where she worked regular shifts, doing something with packaging and sealant, filling boxes with envelopes. She introduced me to the other women who worked there. Everyone smiled. And then I left her there and walked away—but to where? I keep the image of a red-edged window, looking through it to see my mother starting her work. Paper, envelopes— of course it was too much, too obvious. I had held the envelope containing the letter she had sent my dad all those years ago from Pennsylvania. I had taken note of her handwriting, the blue ink. But not the letter itself. That was gone and who can say when or how such artifacts slip away and disappear, lost in the shuffle of our lives. Ten years later, that paper factory went out of business and my mother stopped working altogether. She now spends most of her time in her apartment, where she does not have email or a computer. She has a cell phone, but she doesn't text. The only number I have for her is for a landline, a word that is in use only because *phone* has been wrested into a different meaning of portability. *Landline* is a reminder of the ground, of earth itself, and how odd it seems to be affixed to one physical place.

On another day, I got out of that apartment complex by saying I would take my niece to see Boston while my nephew went to play with friends. Someone must have dropped us off at the nearest T station, and we must have changed trains to the Green Line to get to Back Bay. I didn't know anything about Boston except how to read a map, and that Lily had said I should walk down Newbury Street and check out the shops on the way to the Public Garden. So that's what my niece and I did. We took our time, stopping for ice cream and looking at beautiful clothes. I bought my nephew a shirt and my niece a dress that she wore right out of the store. It was a humid August day, but we kept walking until she complained she was tired.

Back at the apartment, my mother came over for dinner. I was heading back to the Midwest soon, starting grad school in a couple of weeks at the same place I went to undergrad because they'd offered me a full fellowship and stipend. I didn't have a massive amount of loans, but going to grad school right away meant I wouldn't have to start paying them back yet. I was ready to return to my own schooling, ready to be alone in the apartment that I was still paying for because I hadn't found a summer subletter for the two months I was away. My bank account had just enough to get me to my first paycheck as a TA.

We ate dinner while watching television and I knew

this was a chance to ask my mother questions that had been on my mind since long before I had met her. During our first visit, she hadn't been able to tell me when I was born. Couldn't recall. And I had not asked what I really wanted to know, which was how she and my dad had met, and what had happened between them. I wasn't afraid of her in the way I'd been afraid of my dad and his temper, growing up, but I was still afraid of intruding into spaces that were not mine.

At last I found an opening by asking about my maternal grandmother, my own ba ngoai, who still lived in Saigon. My mother said she was going to see her soon because she was planning a trip to Vietnam in a few months, to stay through the American winter months.

I said something about how it must have been hard to leave her mother.

Oh, we had to leave, my mother said, in her airy, no-nonsense style. It was so bad there. We had no money!

She went on to repeat what she had told me during our first meeting, how weeks after the fall of Saigon she had gone to my grandmother Noi's house and a neighbor told her we had all left for America. You didn't even leave a note, my mother said. No nothing.

That must have been terrible, I said.

I was so sad, she said, but she sounded matter-of-fact.

She turned to scold my niece and nephew about something, perhaps to change or end the subject.

It finally occurred to me that maybe this was all that my mother could say, and that this was the only way she could speak of what she had been through.

Maybe I didn't know how to be close to anyone unless I knew it was fleeting, unless I knew I was about to be somewhere else. I was a college graduate when neither my mother nor my dad had finished high school, but I was, in so many ways, profoundly uneducated. Had I ever even said the word *refugee* to Jodi and Lily? No, I wouldn't have because I didn't, back then. I had so much to learn and no understanding of how to begin.

Soon enough I was back at Logan Airport, where my half brother worked for a while as a bus driver. On the plane, I leaned against the window and closed my eyes. I don't know how my mother and I said good-bye. If we hugged. If we made promises to call, to talk, to visit—nothing that would be kept. The summer was over. I would land in Detroit and catch the shuttle to Ann Arbor. I would make my way back to my garden-level apartment where, a few months later, I would watch snow accumulate at the windows. I would unlock my doors and lock them again. I had no television then, no radio, no internet at home. Just a bed, and books, and someone else's sofa. This was before cell phones, before Wi-Fi. None of my friends, not Jodi or Lily either, because not even this friendship would last forever, and no one in any part of my family would know where I was, or how long it had taken to get there.

6

APPARENT, PART III

My sister and I have been in the same room with our mother, all of us together, three times that I can remember.

1.

A confession: I did not tell the whole story of what happened that summer I had a teaching fellowship. Because what really happened is that my half brother, my mother's second child, got married a few days after I finished the fellowship, on a day that he and his fiancée had chosen many months before. Because I was already in Boston, I went to the wedding. And because I went so did my dad, stepmom, and sister, all driving out from Michigan. It was the first time my sister Anh and I saw our mother at the same time and it was the first time I saw our father and mother together in the same place.

I retain tiny details, conversations, and dinners from childhood, yet I have forgotten almost everything about the occasion of my half brother's wedding. The images in my mind are stilled: me in a dress with yellow flowers on it, sitting on my niece's or nephew's bed, waiting, while Anh sits on the other bed. Worrying that our dresses are too casual, that we should have brought or bought something prettier or showier for a Vietnamese wedding. This would be confirmed later on at the reception, in the banquet room of a Chinese restaurant, where everyone else wore shimmering gowns and ao dais.

Recently, I asked my sister what she recalled of that wedding. She said that the duck at the banquet was the best duck she'd ever had. She said she remembered thinking that we had worn the wrong dresses.

She said, It seemed like Mom and Dad didn't want us to be alone with our mother, like maybe they were afraid of what she would say if they weren't around.

This is the verbal construction we use, that we are used to: we refer to our stepmom and dad as "Mom and Dad" in the same sentence as "our mother."

The first time our dad and our mother had seen each other in the United States, Anh was there because that's when she had met our mother, too. I was between my first and second years of college, taking summer classes and working at a reception desk where the manager refused to give me time off, which was fine by me because I hadn't wanted to go to Boston. My sister thought it would be easier to see our mother in a group, but I didn't want anyone to see me seeing my mother. I would wait, to avoid this next level of self-consciousness. Later, when I asked Anh how it went and what it was like, all she said was that it was okay. A little weird. No one had spent much time together, anyway. It had been a relief to hear that. After all, sensational reunions only happened in the worst movies.

At my half brother's wedding, my dad and my mother did not dance together. It wasn't that they avoided each other. But maybe they, too, were conscious of an audience. If they talked, I suspected they did so on their own time. They were, to anyone who knew them, simply people who had a history, with children born of that history.

Sometimes what seems like silence, so large that there is no piercing it, is actually privacy.

When my sister and I, together, met our mother in Boston, before our half brother's wedding, someone took pictures: our mother in the middle, all three of us smiling.

We had few words beyond the usual: How is school? Do you get good grades? As the years went on that would become, Are you working today? Do you work a lot? I don't have any of the pictures that were taken; instead, I think of Anh and me in our niece and nephew's room. Sitting in our wrong dresses on the edges of different beds, waiting to be told what to do next. Were the bedspreads truly pink, or were the sheets pink, or did I only imagine this? Did we talk much? I looked out the window, at the parking lot. My sister and I, like our niece and nephew, had shared a bedroom throughout our childhood, on into high school. When we were very little and slept in the same bed, sometimes we lightly scratched each other's back, making drawings the other had to guess. Later we would sing pop songs from our separate twin beds until we fell asleep. It was so odd, in the morning, never knowing when sleep had overtaken us. What words or notes had been last.

2.

It was about ten years after our half brother's wedding when my sister and I saw our mother again, together. By then, both Anh and I had gotten married, too, and with our husbands had planned a summer week at a free, borrowed house on

Martha's Vineyard. We went in determined vacation mode to ride bicycles, eat lobster, go to the beach, walk around little shingled towns. Anh says it was my idea to take a day trip to Boston to see our mother, which involved a ferry, a bus, a train, and a taxi and took about three hours each way. According to my sister, I made all the arrangements and even called our mother on the phone to tell her that we were visiting. Why did you do all that? Anh asked when I called her recently to see what she remembered of that trip. I said, Because I thought we should tell her we had both gotten married. Oh, she said. Yeah, I guess that makes sense. You always felt worse about that than I did.

It's a point we have never figured out, never agreed on: What do we owe our mother, and how much?

We hadn't told our mother about our weddings because it was simpler not to. I justified it by saying she wouldn't have gone anyway; except for casinos, and her trips to Vietnam, she didn't like to travel. And it would have been an expensive hassle for the Boston family to attend our two weddings in the Midwest. But the harder truth is that a wedding is already a precarious mixing of family with friends. A wedding is all about witnessing. The last thing I wanted was to have my relationship with my mother witnessed, to feel the curiosity of my in-laws' gaze, to have to explain who everybody was. So I took the easy way out.

In Boston that summer day, my mother, half sister, and niece and nephew greeted us with smiles and hugs. They assessed our husbands and laughed and said things like, Oh, he is tall; Oh, he looks a nice man. No one said a word about the weddings. We all crowded into my mother's living room. The television was on—a Vietnamese soap—and in one corner a caged cockatiel hopped around, squawking. I wondered if my mother knew that my dad and stepmom also had a cockatiel, named Baby, who sometimes flew around the house.

My sister and I and our husbands stayed an hour, maybe less. I'm sure we were offered snacks and drinks, and probably declined them. We once again asked and answered the minor questions people trade when they don't know each other very well, and maybe aren't trying to. How is work? we all asked. We are always asking each other about work. Do you like where you live? they asked. How hot is it where you live? What's the weather like? How about babies soon, what do you think? My sister's husband and my own husband, both white guys, did their best small talk. They asked about the pet bird. They asked about living in Boston. They asked my niece and nephew about their schools, their friends, how they spent their summers. At some point, we all fell silent and just looked at the television. In the photos I've kept from that day, my mother looks so small standing next to her three daughters. I'm in a light blue T-shirt and a floral skirt and Anh looks tanned from the beach. My half sister has curly hair and sharper facial features; it's hard to tell that we are related. And then we all said good-bye in the same way we said hello, with big smiles and hugs. It's like we have an agreement about time: just a small amount, just enough to say we saw each other, and that is enough.

The bus line between Boston's South Station and Woods Hole was called Peter Pan, and I slept most of the way. At the dockside we had to wait awhile for the next ferry, which turned out to be the biggest one in the fleet, the one that could hold what seemed an improbable number of cars. We watched them, one after another, drive out of and into the maw. Then we boarded with the rest of the foot passengers and headed to the snack bar. I expected my sister to make a comment about how much time we'd spent traveling for such a short visit, but all she said was, Well, now you can feel better about everything.

But I didn't. I never did. I felt what I had always felt: suspended, stuck. Uncertain of what I was supposed to do but certain that I was doing it wrong.

Anh and I ordered a cup of chowder to share, with an extra packet of oyster crackers. We were quiet, still sleepy.

In a couple of days we'd be back on this boat, returning to Boston, aiming for the airport. We would not talk about our mother again for a long time.

3.

Five years later, Anh and I were both living in Chicago when I convinced her to go to Boston again with me. I'd been invited to give a talk at a library there and figured we could land early and visit our mother before the event. We could eat seafood and stay at a pretty hotel. Just us, I said. Thirty-six hours. No husbands.

We flew from O'Hare to Logan, and even though she'd flown many times, Anh suddenly grabbed my arm as the plane descended toward the runway. I was surprised; it was our dad who had a fear of flying, not her. It's all water, she said. Look, we're going to land in the water; what if we land in the water? I told her we were not going to land in the water. She kept her hand on my arm and said, At least we're together. She didn't let go until all the wheels were touching the runway.

A cousin, David—one of our uncle's kids—was now living in Boston for grad school and he offered to drive us to the apartment complex where my mother lived. I called to tell her we were on our way, and when we arrived she was standing at the edge of the parking lot, as if waiting for us. She was dressed up: satin pants, heels, sparkling jewelry, a tidy black-haired wig. Anh and I got out of the car and she greeted us with hugs, a rush of words saying, You girls are getting too grown-up. Where are your husbands? Are you ever going to have babies? Oh, look at you.

Then she stepped back, done. Okay, she said, Listen. I have to go now.

What? I said. You're going somewhere right now?

I'm going out, she said, as if I'd asked an inane question. She gestured at her clothes. The shine of the satin, of the jewelry.

She told me and Anh to wait out here for our niece, who was still getting ready. I go now, she said. Bye, my girls! She gave another hug, told us to call her, and then walked away. We watched her round the corner of her apartment building. She hadn't said where she was going.

Anh gave me a look that I knew to read as, Well, what did you expect?

David sat in his car, waiting, with a question on his face. We shrugged. We all waited. Soon enough our niece appeared. In the five years since we'd been here, she had grown from a girl into a real teenager in a tank top and denim miniskirt. Somehow Anh and I had not thought to anticipate this. Our niece walked with a kind of swagger, flipping her long hair as if to say that she knew she was pretty and she was tough, too, and what did we think of that?

In fact, she was mad. She stopped in front of me and Anh—we were still standing in the parking lot—and said, Where have you been all these years?

Anh and I looked at each other. We had absolutely no answer.

Our niece—I will call her Jenny now—got into David's car with us and continued her forthright questions. How come you guys don't visit more often? How come you don't call? We never hear from you.

Anh sat in the front and I knew she was trying to avoid Jenny's questions by discussing traffic with David. In the back, all I could do was apologize. She was right: my sister and I had not done enough, had not tried enough.

I had known for some years that my dad and stepmom still sent checks to my mother, calling once or twice a year to see how everyone was doing. My mother had mentioned this, too.

But Jenny was living a different reality, the second-generation experience of being the go-between, shifting from Vietnamese to English, from home to school. Her brother was younger and didn't have half the chores she did; he spent most of his time at his friends' houses; their parents were always working. It was a summer evening and Jenny could have chosen her friends, could have chosen a date, but she felt responsible, and she felt that she should see us, her family, instead. Or so I read into her words. I thanked her for seeing us and I meant it. By the time we reached the library, she had softened enough to smile. She never went to this part of the city, she said. She was curious.

The event was a reading and Q&A and I remember wondering what Jenny was thinking, and if she would tell her parents and grandmother about this, and, if so, how she would describe it. I rarely talked about writing with anyone in my family, or with anyone who wasn't also writing. I was still self-conscious about creative work, like the twelve-year-old girl I once was, wondering if anyone actually wanted to see the painting I had done or if any attention was just indulgence. After it was all over, we stepped out into the warm evening and Jenny said, That was kind of interesting.

We went to a tapas restaurant off Newbury Street where, all those years earlier, Jenny and I had walked, looking in shop windows. My sister and I ordered too much food and talked about the future: college, where did Jenny want to live, what did she want to do. David talked about all the schools in the Boston area. Anh talked about the business she was in, marketing. I encouraged Jenny to seek out subjects she enjoyed, and try new ones, just to see. Jenny, receiving all this advice, wasn't sure about any of it. She wasn't crazy about school and she was bored a lot. She said she wanted to have *fun*.

Just be careful, Anh said, and David and I both looked at her because we knew what she meant. She sounded like our stepmom, who would say that very line to mean *don't get pregnant, don't drop out of school, don't throw everything away for some guy.*

Jenny was more focused on the tapas, the garlicky shrimp and the fried potatoes. She said, This is one of the best meals I've ever had.

Are you going to call me? she asked later when David was driving back to the apartment complex. Are you going to send emails? Are you going to be better about everything?

Yes, I said. We'll be better.

From the front seat Anh said, How about you, Jenny? Are you going to call us? Are you going to stay in touch?

Yeah, she said. And that was the agreement we said good-bye on, the three of us saying that we would call more, and email more, and stay in touch.

Later, in the hotel room my sister and I shared, washing our faces and getting ready for bed, Anh was irritated about our mother. It's just so typical, she said. We fly out here and she's got her own thing anyway. Where was she even going?

I figured it must have been a party, or maybe a date.

Though didn't she already have a boyfriend? Neither of us could remember how serious that was. Obviously, Anh said, wherever she was going was more important than seeing us.

She was irritated about Jenny, too. Why are we supposed to do everything? she said. They never call us. Not ever.

I think we really wanted to mean it when we said we would keep in touch. And we did try. We sent emails, we sent gifts. But my sister and I knew how to make promises—yes, we would send photos to our mother, yes, we would call soon—while knowing we were likely to break them. Because, sometimes, in the moment, you feel a glimmer of what you think you should be feeling. You want to be a certain kind of person, a better person. You want to do better. But you aren't, and you won't, because it is easier, in the end, to keep your distance. You let what is unraveled stay unraveled. Maybe you don't want to be drawn in. You want to preserve yourself, protect yourself. You know the safety of the shore.

———

That moment in the parking lot with my sister and our mother? The three of us haven't been together in the same space since then. A couple of years later, Anh had a baby. A year after that, I had a baby, too. About a decade would pass before either of us would visit our mother again.

When I brought my first son to Boston, when he was a

year old, I had wanted Anh and her child to come along, too, so we could introduce our kids together. She didn't want to go. That was her explanation. A tired sigh: I don't want to. Later, when I admitted that our mother hadn't shown up, she had said, See what I mean?

When you have a sister, and are lucky enough to get along with her, even through teen years of stealing each other's clothes and vaguely resenting whomever the other is becoming, you hone a language of weathering and understanding that no one else can know. When we were in elementary school and she saw someone being mean to me, she would threaten to beat them up, and would have done it. When she was in college and out of money, too far from her next paycheck, she called me instead of our parents. We don't tell each other all of our secrets and confessions—we are sisters, not best friends—but we share an intimacy of space that, as the years go on, seems almost sacred to me. I am comfortable around my sister, can say things with my sister, in a way that I've never been, or will be, with anyone else in the world.

When we were growing up we almost never spoke about our mother, following the unspoken dictate of our household. As we have gotten older, as we've had children of our own, we bring up the subject of our mother more often, more easily. As in, How long has it been since you talked to her? Do you think you'll visit her at some point? Should we go see her in Boston? Slowly, we have brought a once-forbidden topic out into such greater light that now it almost feels normal, almost natural. Hey, we might say, when's the last time you talked to our mother?

Once, I asked Anh why she didn't feel any differently about our mother, now that she knew what it was to be a mother, too. Yeah, she said, I do know. That's why I think she should call *us*. She never makes any effort. What kind of mother is that? This was when our kids were little, at a Christmas get-together at the cottage-like house in Michigan. Anh and I were alone in the kitchen, taking a break from the music in the party room that our dad had built and renovated, and where everyone was hanging out. Anh was looking in the refrigerator, reorganizing the plastic tubs of leftovers. I was thinking about how we had both left this tucked-away house to go to college and had never lived here again. Slowly, my dad was fixing up every room himself. He had replaced the long-ago linoleum, had installed new cabinets and a faux-stone countertop. All the dark-wood paneling was gone.

Can you imagine, my sister said, not wanting to visit or call or talk to your own kids?

But, I said, can you imagine it the other way around, too?

She closed the refrigerator, talking about what her kid, who was in a picky phase, was going to eat. I knew she didn't want to discuss our mother anymore. Back in the party room,

Anh's child climbed into her lap and my sons climbed into mine. They were too little to remember, too young to ask the big questions.

When I was a kid, I thought Christmas was an American holiday. Grown-ups told me to believe in Santa Claus, so I did. And I believed that what I secretly wished for could be made real. I once wrote a letter to Santa, addressing the envelope to the North Pole, and went outside on a blustery day and threw it into the air. I was certain the letter would be carried off, my small dreams (dolls, clothes, money) certain to be answered. A few days before Christmas, I found the letter, sodden, in the bushes next to our ranch house. On Christmas morning, I realized that the gifts that said *From Santa Claus* were written in my stepmom's handwriting.

These are the things that my sister and I laugh about, that we love to laugh about, remembering our former selves. We have never spent a Christmas with our mother, never even considered it. Not Thanksgiving, not Mother's Day, not any holiday. That's how far away she has been for us.

My dad and stepmom are the go-betweens, checking on her, giving her updates over the years about my kids, about my sister's kid—her other grandchildren. I have always pictured my mother not bothering much with Christmas. A few requisite gifts. Some candy. Drinks. She would give crisp bills to my niece and nephew, the way my grandmother Noi had done for me and Anh and our stepsister and brother. I imagined my mother falling asleep on her sofa in the early afternoon. Her man would have gone out—to work, maybe, or to pick up something at a store. The apartment building would seem especially quiet. My mother would curl up a little, giving in to sleep.

If I called, the ringing would wake her up.

But I wouldn't call.

I didn't call for years.

7

MY MOTHERS

When Gen Xers talk about growing up, we talk about how much freedom we had. The latchkey wildness of days with little or no supervision. But the truth behind that is we usually had a mother, somewhere, looking out for us. My grandmother and my stepmom would tell me and my siblings to go out and play, and we did because we had their permission. And we knew we would return to them. They wouldn't be waiting, exactly, but they would be there. They would be, at some point or another, a sense of home. And that is why we could take off, literally running through the neighborhood, bicycling wherever we could manage, as far into the evening as the light would take us.

My grandmother's name was Thi, but everyone called her Noi. The correct, Vietnamese way I should have referred to her was ba noi, meaning "paternal grandmother." But I grew up knowing nothing about my maternal grandmother, who, like her daughter, was never mentioned. And so ba noi was simply Noi—to everyone. The grandmother. To me, she was also one of my mothers.

Born in 1920, she spent the first third of her life in Hanoi. I would learn about her family's northern identity through her cooking, her ao dais, her pronunciation of certain Vietnamese sounds. Hanoi is where she attended a French academy, where all of her siblings and extended family lived and stayed, and where she married the man who would become the grandfather I would never know. By 1952 they had four sons and a business that my dad and uncles have described as thriving and prosperous, something to do with imports and exports. I think those vague words mean that no one really understood or remembered the particulars, which is also part of the story.

Everyone thought my grandmother was so lucky—four boys! But at some point in the early 1950s her husband was taken away and interrogated. Communists, is how my uncles have described this. The details of what happened to him have never been clear, except that he survived. Noi never spoke of it. But when the 1954 Geneva Accords mandated a north-south division of Vietnam, Noi decided that they should take the chance to leave for Saigon.

My dad has said he recalls being on the ship that took them from the north to the south. He didn't know then that nearly a million people were in the midst of such migration, that they were essentially refugees in their own, now-divided, country. He recalled how poor they were in Saigon, starting over. He recalled that Noi took care of both house and business, making food to sell on a busy street. My grandfather was ill, had never fully recovered from what happened to him in the north. When he died, my dad was six years old.

Noi, now the single mother of four children, kept on making and selling food. She sold cards, games, clothing, and toys, running a little shop from her own home. Meanwhile her sons were growing up, heading toward the war that had always been part of their lives. Is it luck that my grandmother only lost one son to that war?

I have seen the black-and-white photographs from my oldest uncle's funeral. In Vietnam, it is not strange to take such pictures. They are private, for the family, too private to describe. Later they gave a kind of comfort to my grandmother when she was on the other side of the world, unable to visit or take care of her son's headstone.

BETH NGUYEN

My grandmother, dad, and uncles were refugees twice, first in 1954 and then in 1975. My grandmother would live the final third of her life in the United States, in a climate she could not have anticipated. I'm always trying to imagine that choice, which maybe didn't feel like a choice at all but a matter of survival. What it would take to make someone—to make you, to make me—leave everything known? The history of my family is also the history of multiple wars, of colonization, of imperialism, of loss and diaspora. So it is with every Vietnamese family that has found its way to the United States. So it is true of most refugees who have landed here, and it becomes both legacy and unasked-for identity. A journal editor once told me not to use the word *trauma*, that it had become meaningless. I see that point, how the word has become too broad, too popular. But what if it is also accurate? I think of echoes and nightmares. Wells of anxiety that never empty. And so much pretending that everything is all right, everything will be all right.

In the beginning of our life in America, Noi slept on a mattress on the floor with my sister and me. I learned this recently, from an aunt who married one of my uncles. It made sense, because Noi wouldn't have left us to sleep alone like that. But my mind has remembered this as something she only did when we were sick, maybe because I was told later that it was *not* normal to sleep next to your grandmother. I have been told that it's impossible to have memories from age two and a half—that I'm just imagining, or extrapolating based on the few photos we have of that time. Fine. But I see her, I feel her, beside me on the mattress on the floor. She gets up, goes to the creaky French doors that divide this room from the living room, where my dad and uncles are. I shift onto my side, toward my sister who really is asleep, and I am so glad, feel so safe, to hear the voices of my family nearby. Many years later, I would sleep next to my own children and it would feel like one of the only correct things I knew how to do.

Every time I think of those early years—how hard it must have been to start over in a new, cold country, in a language she didn't know—I feel freshly devastated for my grandmother, though I do not know if she felt that herself. Maybe it's merely an imposition of my own Americanness. Every walk in the neighborhood, every venture to the grocery store, every outing to a nearby park, risked encounters with white people who stared with open hostility and curiosity. I came to witness and know those stares, too. Learn English, people said, over and over, with their mouths and with their eyes.

In America, you get points for succeeding, not for trying. Yet Noi navigated refugee life with unwavering grace and a sense of self that I will never achieve. She did not balk, flinch, or back down. She was not ashamed of her face or her body.

She sewed most of her own clothes—loose, flowing pants and tunics for summer, hand-knitted sweaters and vests for winter—and wore ao dais whenever we went out. She would not change her dress for America, just as she would not change her food. Together we would walk through the farmer's market and I would watch her negotiate with nods and shakes of her head. The silver scales would sway as they held the weight of the vegetables she had selected. At home she transformed them into soups and curries and stir-fries, always served with rice.

It isn't sufficient to describe Noi as my grandmother. She was the life force of our family. The engine and the everything. She had made the decisions that governed and determined the rest of our lives: our names, what we ate, how we left, where we ended up.

I didn't realize until I was an adult that my grandmother never said I love you, almost never gave hugs and kisses. But I never once questioned the depth of her love. Besides my children, no one has ever loved me, or will ever love me, the way she did.

———

While my grandmother was raising her children in Hanoi and then in Saigon, on the other side of the world the woman I would one day know as my mom was growing up in a big

Catholic family with eight siblings in a town near the eastern shore of Lake Michigan, where her parents had migrated from Texas and, before that, from Mexico. For years, their living relied on the picking seasons of produce like blueberries and sugar beets, and the factory work involved in canning them. My stepmom was not encouraged to go to college but she did anyway, and she kept going, eventually getting a master's degree in education. She moved to Grand Rapids, was a single mom raising a young daughter. One night, this was 1977 or 1978, she and her best friend went to a party where they ended up meeting my dad and one of my uncles. A year or so later, she married my dad. A year or so after that, her best friend married my uncle.

Four decades later, I will call my mother in Boston during the pandemic and she will tell me that my dad sent a letter to her in Saigon, all those years ago, to say he was marrying someone else. That he needed someone to take care of me and my sister. And him.

It's astonishing, or maybe I mean it's moving, to imagine my dad taking the time, the care, the trouble, to write a letter explaining what he was going to do.

Did he write her later, to say that he and his new wife had had a child, a boy? Would he have done that?

When I refer to "my mom" in real life, people who don't know me always assume she's Vietnamese, too, as if I were talking about my mother in Boston instead of the mom I grew up with. Many times I have relied on this assumption as a way to avoid follow-up questions. It wasn't shame. It was me trying to learn the difference between those who asked out of curiosity and those who asked toward understanding.

It was my stepmom who got us out of that first rental house and into the house on Florence Street that had a plum tree and a real backyard that sloped down to a rusting swing set the previous owners had left. She enrolled us in school. She took us to the dentist. She got us doctor's appointments and vaccinations. Maybe these sound like simple, obvious things, but they only are if you know about them and know how to do them. They are the logistics that can make or derail entire years and lives, and it is no surprise that they're usually managed by a mother.

My aunt told me that my stepmom also put a stop to Noi and Anh and me sharing a mattress on the floor. On Florence Street, Noi had her own bedroom and Anh and I shared a room with our stepsister. Even so, Anh and I often slept in the same twin bed after lights-out, until she decided she was too old for such things. Then I started sleeping in my grandmother's room. Not all the time. But my sisters often crowded me out with their clothes and giggles and what increasingly seemed like the foreignness of their lives involving boys and secrets and waiting for certain songs to play on the radio so they could record them. Noi's room had a closet with enough space for me to settle with my books. She had a foam-filled chair that folded out into a narrow pallet bed, its navy-blue fabric dotted with tiny diamond shapes. In the morning all I had to do was flip it back into its chair shape and it was satisfying, like the bed had never been, like the night had never happened.

⸺

We lived in a conservative town, but my stepmom was never afraid to put pro-Democrat signs on the front lawn. She campaigned for Jimmy Carter and later for Mondale/Ferraro. She once brought us kids with her to a picket line when the public schools went on strike, so we, too, could join. I learned the word *boycott* at a young age, though I had to figure out on my own that it wasn't about boys. For years, it seemed, we couldn't eat grapes or lettuce. Never cross the picket line, she would tell us. And don't be a scab. Her favorite book was *The Grapes of Wrath* and it became one of mine, too.

Once, in third or fourth grade, I asked her what I should write down on a homework assignment that told me to list my parents' occupations. Write down that I'm a teacher, she said, because she worked in education. For my dad, she told me to write "blue-collar worker." The phrase stuck in my mind, and I pictured my dad wearing a blue-collared shirt, which he never did. What did that have to do with working at the feather factory? My stepmom said it was just a term used to describe that kind of work. Other kinds of work, she said, were called white-collar.

When I think about that moment with my stepmom, the defining of terms, of work, of metaphor, I think about how careful we all had to be. If I asked too many questions about anything—where was my dad going, why are there so many different kinds of churches—she would say, none of your business. There were a hundred subjects that we had to avoid, like sex, and the war, and the story and whereabouts of my mother. Maybe when you're trying hard to balance colliding worlds, it seems safer if the kids don't know too much, safer to change the channel if actors on the screen start to kiss. Look away, she would tell us.

But that was a hard ask in those deep-eighties days when the television seemed like primary source material. Not just the nightly news but all the commercials, all the sitcoms, all the moments that revealed how people maybe really lived, or so it seemed. I watched television the way I read books: studying, memorizing, looking for clues. As if every cultural product were a puzzle, and the solution—knowledge—would transform me from quiet, shy girl to worldly insider.

If it felt like I was always waiting for something, it's because I was. Waiting for the next episode of *The Facts of Life* and hoping it wasn't a rerun; waiting to be old enough to see R-rated movies that promised so much shock and scandal; waiting for magazines to arrive in order to see something new, something pretty, anything from elsewhere. My uncles subscribed to *National Geographic* and, like most families back then, kept each issue, the stacks of them accumulating in the basement, all those yellow spines facing out. Sometimes we also got *Time* or *Newsweek*, back in their heyday. *Better Homes & Gardens* would appear in the mailbox, or *Popular Mechanics*, because my stepmom had a hard time turning down a good discount rate from a student selling subscriptions door-to-door. I was always bothered by *Better Homes & Gardens*. Was it a challenge to be better than your neighbors, your friends, or your own self? The pictures of perennial-stuffed gardens and serene kitchens told me that it was not meant for blue-collar families. It was meant for moms, white moms, who stayed home because they could, and who had enough money to spend on making sure everything matched. I touched the gloss of the pages, admiring dramatic perfume ads, knowing I was a mere onlooker. In our ranch house no amount of pitching in to clean could change the worn-down rooms. Too many shoes near the front door, too many newspapers and empty cereal boxes in the dining area. The rips and holes in the living room sofa were patched with duct tape, and the off-white walls and popcorn ceilings would never get repainted.

Too often, I thought of my stepmom in terms of ways she failed me. She wouldn't bake cookies for me to contribute to a holiday cookie exchange at the school. She wouldn't sign the permission slip for me to go on a field trip to tour the Kellogg factory in Battle Creek. She wouldn't get us brand-name clothes or shoes. She wouldn't buy Doritos because they were too expensive. I thought of her as the one always saying no to everything, and never stopped to consider why.

But there was one thing I could almost always get: a trip to the local public library. Many weekends and summer days she'd drop us kids off, sometimes just me, and not come back for hours. I never worried about time, or snacks, or being alone. I never felt unsafe at the library. I was at my happiest in a place where nobody was going to roll their eyes at me for reading too much, where the whole purpose of the place was finding and reading books, and where people were required to be quiet. My stepmom didn't approve of borrowing a lot of books at once because she was sure that I would lose or forget them. And I did rack up some overdue fines. But she would relent and mutter that I would have to pay with my birthday money or Tet money. On the car ride home, I would cradle stacks of books on my lap, deciding which needed to be read first.

All the self-consciousness I carried around about my face, my race, about all the feelings I didn't have a language for—all that vanished when I was among books. I loved to see the little due date card tucked into the pocket inside each book. A visible, stamped history of other people's readings. The cards kept their own measure of time—how often or seldom a book was chosen by someone—and I could never look at them without feeling the pang of some vague loss. The end or return of a book was like the end of a friendship.

I recently went back to see the district branch we went to most often. The building has been remodeled, even the façade altered so that whatever I remembered, experienced, no longer exists. But the feeling is still there. I know in my mind the color of the bricks lining the walkway to the door; I know the tile flooring in the atrium and the clear view to the circulation desk with the librarians who would always ask if they could help. There used to be a stand near the entrance that held the largest dictionary I'd ever seen. Waiting for my stepmom to pick me up, I would read whatever page was open. I'd turn to another page, at random, and read the words on it. Always an astonishment, how many meanings I didn't know and how many I would never know. And I would wonder how many people, just like me, did the same thing, searching for words and meanings they would never retain.

I didn't know it then, didn't appreciate it, but my stepmom was saving my life. It would be many years before I would see that the point of home is that it is a known space. More and more, that house on Florence Street is the one I dream about. Did we really only live there seven years? By the time we left, my dad and stepmom and uncles had replaced the broken chairs and gotten a new sofa, the puffy kind, covered in velvet-like corduroy, the exact color of the canned mushrooms my stepsister loved. My stepmom found a mid-century credenza at a secondhand shop. My dad replaced the kitchen linoleum with tile. They did what they could, when they could. It's one of those things I didn't realize until long after it happened.

———

When I was a kid we almost never went to Lake Michigan even though it was less than an hour's drive away. We would go, instead, once or twice a summer, to one of the sad inland lakes nearby, where any sense of beach was just pebbles and grass. I never got in those waters. I would sit with my books and eat potato chips and wait for the hours to pass so we could go home. Everyone else in my family loved the water. I had a fear of it—I still do—and it took me years to learn how to swim. My dad said that I'd fallen into the water when I was a baby and that's probably why I was afraid. But his story shifted a bit whenever he said this—it was a river, it was the sea. So who knows.

I only learned how to swim because the lessons were built into our gym classes. It was called Drownproofing. The elementary school had the unusual feature of an indoor swimming pool that was also wheelchair accessible, something I had never seen before and have hardly seen since, designed to facilitate physical therapy. All of this seems incredible to me now, and I cannot imagine such a thing being possible in my children's schools today. But I happened to go through elementary school during a brief, golden moment of American public education that was shaped by the civil rights movement and later the Carter administration, and not yet cut away by the policies of the late Reagan era. So once a week I endured the embarrassment of changing into a swimsuit in a locker room and then getting into pool water that was never quite warm enough. Drownproofing meant learning what to do if your boat tipped over, including how to make a life jacket out of a pair of pants. It meant a lot of treading and swimming. While my classmates learned the crawl, the breaststroke, and the butterfly, I held on to a kickboard for what might have been years.

Access to swimming was one of the earliest markers of class that I perceived. You either went swimming in lakes and pools during the summer, or you didn't. Even if my dad and stepmom had been able to afford it, they never had the time, and my grandmother Noi didn't drive. It was only after I had kids that I understood how much work and privilege is involved in planning, in thinking ahead, in getting them to the milestones you hear they're supposed to reach.

My dad would talk about all the swimming and fishing he did in Vietnam, but the fishing rods he kept in the garage didn't seem to get used. It was my stepmom, of course, who took action. From the perspective of my childhood self, my parents decided to put an aboveground swimming pool in the backyard. From the perspective of my parenting self, my stepmom figured she could bring water to us far more easily, and safely, than she could bring us to the water.

It was a good move that took us through two summers, Noi checking on us from the kitchen window. We filled the pool with water from the hose, which seemed to take forever, and then we had to wait forever for the sun to warm it up. That pool was my kind of non-swimming. I could stand up and the water wouldn't go past my chin. My siblings and I, with our friends, would float for hours, singing songs from the American Top 40 countdown. I can still hear us shouting the words to "Electric Avenue," "Karma Chameleon," "Gloria,"

"Owner of a Lonely Heart." *Much better than owner of a broken heart.* Sometimes we'd move in a circle together to create a whirlpool effect, and let the current tug us along. Then one day I overheard one of my stepsister's friends say the pool was trashy. I already knew it was nothing compared to an actual in-ground pool. But somehow the word still hurt. When cool weather arrived, my dad and stepmom would pull a tarp over the giant tub. I would have to see it the rest of the fall and winter and well into spring, blanketed, collecting leaves and rain and snow.

Noi almost never went swimming, though unlike me she wasn't scared of it. She preferred to keep an eye on things while knitting at the same time. She would sit with her left ankle balanced on her right knee, her reading glasses just so in order to measure her progress on the sweater she was making for the coming winter. In Michigan, no matter how warm it got, the promise of cold weather was never far off.

On the very hottest days of each summer, when my mind returns to the waters of my childhood, I don't think of the murk of inland lakes or the expanse of Lake Michigan on the rare times we saw it, pretending it was an ocean. I think of running through the sprinklers in the backyard, and treading water in the aboveground pool. And I think of a strange shallow wading pool, made of concrete so rough it seemed deliberate, that once existed near the elementary school. One step too fast and your foot would be scraped raw. Maybe it had been built for heat wave days, though we didn't have many. Back then, most people where we lived didn't have air-conditioning units. We didn't. If a summer night got too hot and muggy, we'd go camp in the basement that my dad had finished himself, with a Ping-Pong table, built-in shelves for games and toys, and burnt-orange carpeting. That concrete wading pool was almost always empty. A rectangle just slightly dipped into the ground, with a large, creepy-looking drain in the middle. Once, Anh and I happened to be walking by when water suddenly started coursing into it, from an opening on one side. We went over to watch. There was no telling who or what controlled the water. Other kids came by, then ran to tell others. Soon a small crowd grew. Other kids started to take off their shoes and flip-flops. At last Anh and I did the same, stepping carefully so as not to cut our feet. The water had the smell of the water that came from the garden hose. It swirled up, so cold, just past our ankles. I wondered the whole time—I am still wondering—where it was coming from.

I am such a long distance from the country of my birth, such a distance that the fact of it seems to become more and more an abstraction. A story. I am a long distance, even, from the backyard that shows no trace of the pool that once sat there. From that concrete pool that has been so erased from the actual earth that I could not begin to find where it was.

If I say too often that I am lucky, it's because I am scared of taking anything for granted. I am lucky to have grown up with my grandmother Noi, who was always there when I left for school and always there when I returned, and lucky to have my stepmom to provide a sense of stability in our household. After my dad lost his job at the feather factory, he never really worked a steady, full-time job again. I was starting middle school then, and my dad seemed to spend most of his time hanging out at Saigon Market or at his friends' houses, usually gambling, always drinking. Many nights he wouldn't return until the rest of us were asleep. What I see now is that we were all trying to figure out how to be, or how to grow up. But we didn't know how to say it, didn't know how to talk to each other. And so a cloud of our own making descended over our household, and we learned to live in it.

The cloud followed us to the exurb and the cottage-looking house. Sometimes, as if searching for peace, to get away from the small space I shared with my sister, I would go sleep next to my grandmother. She had a queen-sized bed and she always slept with her head facing Buddha, as was proper, though anyone who didn't understand this would say she was sleeping in the wrong direction. I would almost always go to sleep later—as late as possible, to finish homework and then to have some house-quiet to myself, a habit that has never ended for me. My grandmother would sometimes stir a bit as I settled next to her. She was, in sleep, as she was in life: respectful, aware of space, and generous. She would share anything she had.

Only after both of my sisters went away to college did I settle back into the doorless room that Anh and I had shared. Alone, I spread out my clothes and papers, taking up every available surface. I grew messier, lost track of homework assignments, was always misplacing the T-shirt or pants I wanted to wear. I, too, slept in what others would say was the wrong direction, my feet facing the window. Not out of any sense of respect but out of habit, like saying good night to my grandmother after brushing my teeth. I had enough sense by that point to want to be like her, and enough sense to know that I would never succeed. Years after I, too, went away to college, my dad would demolish part of that A-frame space; I would come home to visit and see the living room ceiling reach all the way to the top, my former bedroom turned into a little loft with a balcony.

Many years after that, my dad would drain and cover

the in-ground swimming pool that had once beckoned us to the cottage-looking house. He'd build a dance floor over it. He and my stepmom would throw parties and people would dance, not knowing what water had flowed and who had swum beneath their feet. All of us kids would be grown-ups by then, all of us living in other states, treading in other summer pools. My grandmother Noi would have been living with one of my uncles for years at that point, being another mother to his son.

The two women who were not my mother were my most real mothers. When my mother in Boston nods with respect when referring to my ba noi, when she calls her a great lady, when she tells me that my stepmom is a good person, I think she understands this, too. I do not mean any of this as tragedy. I mean it as a kind of fact. As another form of luck.

I can't remember my grandmother ever getting mad, truly mad, at me or anyone. She would scold us, but she never yelled. She was the calmest person I ever knew. I thought she was a perfect being in this way, but as I grew up it occurred to me that maybe it was part of her life's work. That she worked every day, her whole life, to be the person she was. It wasn't some kind of magic or preternatural gift. It was work.

My stepmom, in contrast, didn't hide her anger. When she told us, Use your voice, she meant it. When she said Callate la boca, she meant that, too. She wasn't the default polite midwesterner, though she does like her positive-thinking aphorisms, like the one about how more water lifts up every boat. She has a sign in the living room that says: *Dance.* It's easy to poke fun at this, but when I look back at my childhood, all the time further from the actual experience of it, I see my stepmom truly was trying to lift up all of our boats. I had no appreciation of this because I was too busy looking at everyone else on the sea.

Sometimes, when I'm driving to pick someone up or drop someone off, or fetching the weekend newspaper lying at the end of the driveway, I will see a stranger seeing me and wonder what level of stranger I am to them. How I am, too, a stranger. Who among us is truly loved? Can we ever understand who we were or can we only recall how others were in call-and-response, shaping us? I think of the way my stepsister would talk back, the faces my sister would make, rolling her eyes. They would cross their arms. They would stalk to the bathroom to curl and spray their hair. I am defined by familial and physical proximity, because maybe that's all I knew; that's exactly what I thought I was. I was on the edge, gauging the scene. Whether habit or tactic, it crystallized into a lifelong way of being. And so I see my stepmom then versus how I see her now. I see her as someone I didn't understand, someone I have learned to understand. The failings were mine more than hers. I see now what I never could, then: that she was always trying to be someone's mother.

———

My grandmother Noi has been gone for almost fifteen years. I use the word *gone* because somehow it makes more sense to me than the word *dead*. I do not mean to say that I think she is here, not in a way that implies spiritual understanding or belief. I know she is gone, but at the same time, I do not feel that she has left us. The feeling of who she was to me—safety, care, generosity—stays with me.

The last time I was in Michigan I went to her room, her last bedroom, in my uncle's house. Almost all of her things were still there. Even her underwear, folded in its drawer, her now-vintage shoes wrapped carefully in their boxes. The closet was filled with her clothes—the silken tunics and pants she sewed herself, the vests she knitted. Her dressiest damask and velvet ao dais. Thousand-piece jigsaw puzzles from the eighties, ones I watched her piece together to form a luxurious garden, or a castle somewhere in England, me having only the patience to contribute a few edge sections. My uncle showed me some of her knitting needles, a box of old buttons she had collected, her U.S. passport that she had needed for our one trip to Vietnam. There was a jewelry box filled with tissue-thin letters from Vietnam, tucked into blue-edged airmail envelopes. My uncle put them in my hands, along with her passport. Take as many of her clothes as you can, he said. Take anything you want.

The layout of my uncle's house is eerily similar to that of the ranch house on Florence Street. I had wondered if it was strange for my grandmother to return to such a familiar-looking place. Every time I was there, it was like a palimpsest, one house overlaying another, the short hallway to the bedrooms the same that I once traversed, deciding where I should sleep. And Noi's bedroom here was in the same location, in the corner, one window facing the front and one window facing the side. Even the closet, even the altar, were in the same places. This was the room where my sister and I had gone after Noi's death, where we had found the calendar pages she had kept, affixing our dates of birth. When I was very young, I would ask my grandmother in Vietnamese, every night, if it was okay for me to go to sleep. I don't know how the habit started, but I kept it for years. Sometimes she would laugh and say no, it was not okay. But I wouldn't leave until she granted a form of permission. I had this longing to ask her that, now, one more time. I looked to the altar, to the windows, to the bed, to the clothes in my own hands. No, she was not truly gone. *Grandmother, I'm going to sleep now. Is that okay?*

My children never got to meet Noi but somehow,

strangely, I feel that they know her. They respect and love her. What they will never know is the comfort and mayhem of growing up in a multigenerational family all together in the same house. Instead, we've moved around the country, following academic tracks. Every moment of their care has been handled by their parents or by school or by someone paid to do this work. It is work, no doubt. I do not think we were meant to be alone in it. Yet so many of us Gen X parents are. We, the last group of people to go through childhood without the internet, have understood silence and space in a way that our children never will. We are the ones giving permission now. We are the ones waiting for someone to come home.

8

WHITE MOTHERS

We all have other mothers, but sometimes it takes years to realize who they are. Celia, my high school boyfriend's mother,
was one of mine. The boyfriend and I almost broke up a
dozen times in the years we were together; I'm not sure why
he stayed. But I know why I did: I didn't want to lose Celia.

The boyfriend—let's call him Evan. He was white, like
almost everyone else in my school, and because of all that
whiteness I had figured I wouldn't date anyone until college.
This was before it was mainstream cool or normal or creepy
for white guys to be with Asian girls—at least, where I grew
up. It was considered, instead, an aberration. Something uncomfortable that most midwesterners were too polite to comment on until your back was turned. I knew this because my

sister Anh had dated white guys and gone to school dances with them but didn't hang out with their families. She was pretty and outgoing, though, and I wasn't. She had secret boyfriends; I had secret crushes. I didn't even need more. For me, the pleasure of a crush was about impossibility as much as it was about imagination.

I didn't have a crush on Evan; we were actual friends. He was an honors student who played on the soccer team but wasn't a star, and he was funny in a way that didn't rely on belittling others. There was something steady and safe about him. We were always in the same English classes, so I knew that he did the assigned readings. He knew how to analyze texts and write a strong thesis statement. These were things that impressed me.

After a while, I started looking at Evan as someone who would make an ideal theoretical first boyfriend. It still wasn't a crush, exactly, more like a thought process. Later I felt like I'd willed the relationship into being. He never asked me out. I never asked him. It just sort of happened. When I think of Evan in high school, I see him in a faded red polo shirt with variegated black stripes and a collar gone gray with so many washings. He has round wire glasses and he's writing notes in small, blocky print. Everything about school—homework, class participation, group projects, socializing at lunch—comes easily to him. He is favored not just in English lit but calculus, too, world history, physics. I feel like I have to work twice as hard and still his grades are usually better.

I had first seen his mother, Celia, at an awards ceremony when Evan and I were in eighth grade. She had walked down the auditorium aisle in a way that conveyed the confidence of understated glamour, something that was hard to come by in West Michigan, that probably took generations of comfort to bestow. I don't think she was even aware. I once told her that she reminded me of pictures I'd seen of Jackie Kennedy and she blushed.

Three years later, Evan and I were going out. That's the phrasing we used then, "going out" an elevation from a prior era of "going with." There were about 250 students in my high school class. The very coolest girls dated boys from other schools or even boys in college. I always wondered how they even found each other. This was before I understood how communities are made outside of school, through churches and golf clubs and country clubs and summer camps. Here the students were a lot richer than the families on Florence Street. People had lake houses that they referred to as cottages, located somewhere "up north." I never got over the wasteful abundance of it: a whole other house that was only used in the summer, that just sat there empty the rest of the year? Where, exactly, was "up north"?

Evan and I took the same classes and spent a lot of time

talking about books, about characters fictive and real. My stepsister called us nerds. And we did spend a lot of time on homework and research. We hung out with other friends that my stepsister would have called nerds, too. And sometimes, when Evan didn't have soccer practice, we would take long drives on country roads in a car borrowed from his dad or stepmom. A couple of times we stopped to wade in a creek that ran next to a raggedy field where Evan said that people played polo. All I knew about polo was the shirts that the rich kids wore, with the telltale stitched insignia. It hadn't occurred to me that it was a real thing.

I've thought about that field so many times in the years since. A sudden vast expanse, hedged by willows and cattails and so many trees I hadn't yet learned to name. At times, I wondered if I'd really seen it at all. It was a reminder of how worlds can overlap, even concentrically, yet still seem out of reach or out of sight.

Evan was in one of those unknown worlds. Our relationship would have been improbable if not for the stronger force of proximity. A crush was theory, but proximity was practice. In a high school as small as ours, where the rules of heteronormativity were strict, everyone knew the histories of who'd gone out with whom. John and Yoko, his friends called us at first. I was too embarrassed to say anything back. Eventually, everyone more or less got used to seeing us together.

———

We lived in an exurb that was becoming a suburb, and the landscape showed its bewilderment: old farmhouses neighbored industrial parks and subdivisions named for crests and hills that didn't exist. Celia, Evan's mother, lived on the farthest edge of this exurb in a yellow house on a piece of property large enough for a horse barn. Often Evan and I would go to his mom's after school and on the weekend. We spent the hours the way I'd always imagined spending them: a group of us with our own books, reading; maybe playing a board game; watching and discussing the news or some other show together. Celia had three cats and we were always getting up to let one of them outside or inside. Sometimes Celia went out to garden; sometimes Evan and I wandered around the property. Eventually, we'd all sit down for dinner, and stay there for the full duration of the meal. By the time I graduated from high school, I had spent so much time in Celia's house that I could tell you about every room and how the light came into each one.

If there was such a thing as old white money in this part of America, Celia's family had been in its grasp. While the east side of Michigan made auto and industrialist tycoons, the west side had lumber and furniture barons. Fortunes culled from stolen lands, though I didn't know that then. Celia's parents had grown up in Victorian mansions that are now showpieces, if they haven't been torn down or divided into apartments. I learned this only after I asked about her family, because part of old money, I also learned, was not talking much about it. Part of old money was looking like you didn't necessarily have a lot of money at all, because maybe you didn't, really, anymore.

Not that the phrase "old money" ever came up in my many long talks, years of them, with Celia. Like most authentic people, she inhabited rather than explained. Let me be clear: she was the authentic one and I was the one playing pretend. She moved through the world and I watched to learn how. I'd spent much of my life reading, observing, and studying the lives of white people, in books, on the screen, and in real life. Celia allowed me a view that was so up close, it almost felt like I was invited inside.

———

Both of Evan's parents were on their third marriages; he was the product of their second. Such a circumstance was unheard of in our conservative town, and I liked Evan for this. When he told me that his mom had married a younger man, I knew that I would love her.

Where we lived overlapped with horse country, something I knew nothing about except that there were plenty of what we called horsey girls—girls who had or rode horses, who talked about them, who used *stable* as a verb, who possessed an entire equestrian vocabulary. Horse world, or what little of it I glimpsed, was yet another arena that showcased the differences between rich and poor. There were those who owned horses and those who trained them; there were those who rode horses and those who took care of them. There were racehorses and there were workhorses. There were people who truly played polo.

Evan's dad and Evan's mom were people who owned horses. His dad wasn't old-money—his cars were a little too flashy—but he had real estate and some sort of insurance business. Evan grew up on the horse farm his dad had purchased—bright white picket fences surrounding all—and which, in the weird logic of our exurb, was only a few minutes away from where my family lived, in the hidden cottage-looking house that I had never stopped hating. During the summer, Evan sometimes worked with a group of guys hired to bale hay on the farm. Evan had an excessive amount to say about the merits of baling versus rolling. Whenever I drive through a countryside and see those Swiss rolls of hay sitting in fields as if stopped in mid-push, I think about how rolling might be easier than baling, but the end result is never as good.

Celia was a former horsey girl and I learned that people with money, especially old money, didn't mind getting literal dirt on their hands. They pursued it. They gardened with vigor. They walked through expensive mud. They took very long walks through fields, along dusty paths. Horse world was filled with smells of hay and sweat and shit and mud, and it all took a lot of money to maintain. I learned that even dirt had its hierarchies and there were only certain kinds that people with money were willing to touch.

———

When you're not white but surrounded by people who are, you learn pretty fast how to read a room. I had been doing such reading from my earliest moments of consciousness, and by high school had become expert at gauging a white person's comfort or discomfort around me. That's how I knew that Evan's mother and her husband were comfortable with me and that Evan's dad and his wife were not.

Because Evan shuttled between his dad's and mom's houses, I often compared how they lived. Celia and her third husband, a horse trainer, had a farmhouse, old and preserved enough to have *character* but not so old as to be on the brink of crumbling. (A seventies cottage-looking house did not have such character.) In a hallway there would be an antique table holding a pitcher-shaped vase, into which Celia would drop a handful of snapdragons or tulips cut from the yard. Evan's dad and stepmom had hired an interior designer to outfit their house in a mash-up of western and southwestern styles. This was an era when a lot of white people in the Midwest claimed that they were descended from Sacajawea. Maybe they still do. I recall a suede-covered L-shaped sofa in a family room that no one went into. Glass-topped tables held up by sculptural cones. "Tribal masks" as décor.

Evan's dad was the mansplaining type and the stepmother was cheerful in such an effortful way that any interaction felt exhausting. They focused on the predictable questions—school, school activities, and sports—that Celia had little patience for. Once, I was invited to a Thanksgiving buffet in the faux-southwestern dining room. Evan's dad came over to where I stood in line and put his hands on my shoulders to make me take two steps to the side. He hadn't liked the way I had been standing; he thought I wasn't in alignment with everyone else. There, he said, with a smile as if he'd done me a favor.

I had a secret habit, back then, of writing lists and notes and then tearing them up into tiny bits, to avoid any chance of my sisters reading them. I had adopted this method after years of keeping diaries and journals that, no matter where I tried to hide them, were always found and read by my sisters and stepmom. I had tried writing in the backs of notebooks, as if I could fool anyone with a bunch of blank first pages. I had tried writing in secret code but kept forgetting my own system. It was easier, I found, to write and then destroy.

In high school, some of those lists were about Celia. An approximation:

Cloth napkins at every dinner. Beds always made. Newspapers and magazines in a basket. Plain turtleneck sweaters, without a necklace. Monogrammed stationery.

Before Celia, I had never seen, outside of a TV show, a parent having conversations with their kid that had nothing to do with permission or scolding or rules. Evan and his mother talked about whatever was on their minds, from politics to gossip about distant family members to childhood memories. They laughed together, a lot. Their talk meandered and the meandering was the point. So quickly, so easily, they folded me into this; I was grateful. Celia loved reading, so we often talked about books. She was the one who gave me a copy of Louise Erdrich's first novel, *Love Medicine*. I read it again and again. One of my favorite chapters takes place at a highway weighing station—something I'd seen so many times—and I felt like Celia recognized this in me, this need to connect story with reality. We could spend long afternoons going over passages of a book, thinking out loud about what had happened and what might happen to characters we had come to know. Celia asked questions all the time, but it never felt like she was prying, trying to get to a secret side of me, the way it often did when white people asked questions about my family, as if driven by a colonizing curiosity. When Celia asked what kind of orchids my grandmother grew, and how did she take care of them, or what was my first memory, or what were my parents like, whatever I answered, however openly or reservedly, I knew that she wouldn't hang on to it for judgment or ridicule or future ammunition. Later in life, I realized the enormous generosity of this. It was a kind of freedom, and I didn't even know it.

But mostly, I didn't tell the truth about myself. I never talked about how my family had left Vietnam, or about the way we dealt, or didn't deal, with the aftermath of so much turmoil. No, I was ready to show, instead, that I was more American than anyone else, had known all the state capitals since elementary school, had memorized facts about the Constitution and the Declaration of Independence, had taken a literal test to prove myself worthy of citizenship. I was immersed in the assimilationist, acculturation systems that I had been taught, that would take decades to undo. Celia and Evan knew how my family had come to the United States, but they didn't view me as a refugee any more than I did. That was by design, by my own intention. I had surpassed that label of refugee, surely. It would never have occurred to me that all this fronting was also a condition of refugeeness.

Celia and Evan knew that my mother lived in Boston, but it was easy to make that sound like a choice of immigration rather than an act of resettlement. Someone moves to the United States, ends up in Boston. In their kindness, and their not-knowing, they never pushed for more details.

Being with Celia was also a respite from daily life with my dad and stepmom, whose relationship had become so tense that it was preferable to be anywhere else, do any extracurricular, Model UN, debate team, student activity, than be in that cottage house. Anything could set off a fight: a wrong grocery item; one of us kids forgetting to turn off the stereo. Someone staying up too late to play video games. Someone spilling water, spilling Sprite, spilling cereal. Every day someone was yelling, someone was sulking. My dad would storm off in his burgundy-colored Toyota truck, disappearing up the driveway. Almost always there was something still being hauled in that truck, like planks of lumber, and I would watch the way they rattled around as my dad drove away.

Only Noi remained peaceful. She would walk through

the tension of the house and continue watering her plants. She would prep dinner, making sure the rice was always kept on warm. Nothing interrupted her evenings, not even us, watching TV too loud, barging into her room because we often forgot, were so careless about, the hours she reserved for her meditation. There were times, late at night, or when Evan was out of town, when I would hide out in Noi's room while she meditated. I was no good at it myself, kept trying and failing, but the nearness of my grandmother was a quiet force, or a force of quiet, that helped. I had no clue, then, and maybe none of us did, that we were a family continually being shaped by a past—who we were, how we had gotten here—that would never leave us.

———

One winter, Evan's dad and stepmother invited me along on a family trip to Chicago to see *Miss Saigon*. It was the space between Christmas and New Year's, and Evan and I were back home after our first semesters at different colleges.

I had heard of that musical in the way I'd heard of *The Phantom of the Opera*, but knew little about either. The only theater I'd seen had been school productions. I didn't know how hugely successful *Miss Saigon* had been in New York and London, or that Chicago was its first stop in the touring production. The discomfort I felt about the subject of

Vietnam was the same I'd faced with so many war movies like *Platoon* and *Full Metal Jacket*—the self-consciousness about non-Vietnamese people turning and looking at me. My response, at the time, was always the same: say nothing and pretend not to notice.

We took the Amtrak to Chicago, the first time I'd ever been on a train, and the first time since childhood that I'd been to Chicago, and I sat many miles trying to read a book while listening to Evan's stepmother discuss with her twenty-something daughter what they would wear to the theater. The stepmother said she had brought along a sequined catsuit as an option. I didn't know what a catsuit was and pictured a furry costume. Back then, in the era of grunge, I didn't care about clothes and would wear the same plaid shirt several days in a row. I had nothing fancy and couldn't afford to go buy something. Even though I'd read and reread *The Age of Innocence* with its pivotal theater scenes, it hadn't even occurred to me to ask what I should wear.

Miss Saigon was staged in a theater that Edith Wharton might have approved of. The ceiling of arcing lights, the up-holstered seats, the carpeted aisles the color of actual blood, and the thrilling sight of box seats where countless deals, flirtations, and disappointments surely had gone down. Evan's stepmother wore the catsuit after all and it looked like a bodysuit, or what we called leotards back then, paired with a long velvet skirt. I kept my coat on to conceal my plain pants and sweater.

I was completely unprepared for *Miss Saigon*. And was grateful for the darkness of the theater. Like everyone in America, I had seen plenty of racist Asian stereotypes in movies and shows. Mocking accents. Jokes about eating dogs. *Sixteen Candles*. But it was so much worse when it was live, right in front of me, the reduction of Vietnamese characters into sexualized women and evil men, speaking in broken English. All these years later, I still know the chorus of "The Heat Is On in Saigon": *One of these slits here will be Miss Saigon.*

Based on the also racist *Madame Butterfly* and written by two white men, *Miss Saigon* is about a Vietnamese sex worker but also virgin named Kim who falls in love with a white soldier named Chris. He says he will take her to the United States but ends up leaving without her during the fall of Saigon. A few years later, he returns with his white wife. Kim is now an exotic dancer, which is the phrase that people used back then, and thinks that Chris will bring her and their young son to America. Of course, Chris stays with his wife. In the final scene, Kim kills herself so that the white couple can raise her son as their own.

This was the early nineties. I had one semester of college behind me and a barely nascent sense of awareness about issues of race, racism, and representation. I had dealt with aggressions and micro-aggressions all my life but had rarely spoken about them. I could barely describe them to myself. I was still learning about exoticism and appropriation and the depths of empire and colonization. What I knew, mostly, was the feeling of shame: so familiar, so entrenched, yet I couldn't have explained it if I tried. The shame of the foreigner, who is so easy to dismiss. The shame of knowing the standards and defaults of white beauty, white knowledge, white rules, and feeling the violence of them but not the freedom to name them. There's no subtlety in *Miss Saigon*. Kim must be eliminated so that her half-white son can have an American life with the white man and his white wife. Kim is a sex object, and everything about her life, her body, her story, is disposable.

It was not lost on me that I was in that theater as a guest of my white boyfriend's family. And I had no choice but to watch the whole thing.

I started crying as the show ended. I couldn't stop myself, and it was all so humiliating: the musical and the crying. Evan and his family thought I was moved by *Miss Saigon*, which was unbearable. But I let them think that, because it was easier than saying anything closer to the truth, which I couldn't have articulated anyway. Evan's dad and stepmother had paid for everything—the tickets and the train and the hotel, so all I could say was thank you. I wonder now if they thought they were giving me the gift of a show that was related to my "culture." I wonder if they thought they were somehow helping me.

I don't remember much else about that trip except the cold, and the long walks Evan and I took around downtown, crisscrossing bridges over the Chicago River. He thought *Miss Saigon* was sentimental drivel. I'm pretty sure he used the term *lowbrow*. We never talked about race, Evan and I. We never talked about racism. He didn't bring it up—why would he?—and I didn't either.

Later, back in Michigan at Celia's farmhouse, he recounted the weekend to her. He described the musical, making fun of it. I talked about the dinner we'd had at the Cape Cod Room in the Drake Hotel, though I didn't mention how nervous I'd been. I hadn't thought to bring a dress or skirt, and had not known we were going to such a nice restaurant. Celia said it sounded like a very generous weekend, and I smiled because I knew she meant "extravagant." She rarely said anything derisive about her ex-husband, but she sometimes rolled her eyes. I don't really care for musicals, she said. Evan said he hated them. He'd never wanted to see *Miss Saigon* in the first place, or any Broadway musical for that matter. God-awful, he said. I think I just nodded.

Mostly, I felt exhausted. It would be years before I understood that as the exhaustion of pretense, of trying to navigate white spaces and expectations. Of having no one to talk to about it, and not having any words to convey my jumble of feelings anyway. I didn't even recognize that Celia, too, was part of the system that held whiteness as a goal. I would have told anyone that she was on my side, but what did that mean except that I would always understand her more than she could understand me? For Christmas she had given me a canvas tote bag from L.L.Bean, my initials stitched on the pocket in red. Inside, more gifts, including a set of monogrammed stationery, cream-colored card stock with my initials embossed at the top. I had never had anything monogrammed before. To see my name in that way, the actual words hidden, conveyed instead by initials— *B M N*—felt at once startling and revelatory. It felt exactly like what I was, and where I was: both hidden and unhidden, trying to find some in-between. I had loved these gifts, and only much later recognized that they, too, were emblems of whiteness that I was still learning—that maybe she was trying, even, to help me learn. That she had seen me observing and striving, and wanted to help.

In the months and years to come, I would take out the embossed cards and stare at them. Too beautiful to use. It might be the middle of summer, me sitting alone in the gathering heat of an un-air-conditioned apartment, filled with the strange sense of safety that came from feeling isolated, no one else knowing where I was, and suddenly I'd be thinking about Christmas, thinking about Celia planning her gifts so many weeks in advance. I pictured her tying ribbons and settling the packages just so inside the canvas bag. It had given her pleasure to do this, I know, as it would've given me. And she did know me, then. She knew the life I was studying. She knew that I would save the stationery and that I would keep the monogrammed bag forever, filling it with books or clothes, bringing it with me to beaches or overnight trips. I have kept it with me in every place I have lived since.

I have wished to go back in time, to give my former selves the words they lacked. I have thought, well, would anyone have listened or understood, anyway? And then I have to remember that the words would be for me, not for them.

Assimilation is an old, awful, out-of-date idea. But it defined generations, including mine, and it hasn't disappeared. It's just gotten quieter. Assimilation requires a constant form of gaslighting that we do to ourselves.

———

Sometimes, after Evan dropped me off and I walked up the steps to that cottage-looking house, I could almost feel myself shape-shifting, going back to the girl my family knew.

The nerdy one, the weird one. Too big for your britches, my stepmom would say. It came to me that everyone in my family could see how much I wanted to be somewhere else—anywhere else—and if they resented me for it, how could I fault them? Pausing just outside the front door that Christmas break, after *Miss Saigon*, I could see the multicolored lights from the same fake Christmas tree we'd unfolded and folded for years, and it almost made a convincing picture: nightfall, clear sky with Orion. The possibility of snow. The little window in the top of the A-frame was dark. As always, I could smell my grandmother's incense before I stepped inside. I was a little tired of it, to be honest. The way it seeped into my clothes, into every fabric in the house. In fifteen years my grandmother would die on the winter solstice. It would take me that long—longer—to form an understanding of my family, our silences, our shared years, all that we'd been through without ever talking about it.

Evan never came over to my house. None of my friends did. I was embarrassed by the undone rooms that my dad kept starting to renovate but never got close to finishing. I didn't want anyone to see the little doorless room I had shared with Anh, our twin beds divided by a dresser that was so old, it left wood shavings on our clothes with every opening and closing of the drawers. Most of all, I didn't want to face any questions: about how we lived, about Buddha and his altar, about my grandmother and her meditation. All of that tapped into a different feeling—something like privacy. A sense of protection. Evan, and other boys after him, described me as withholding. It wasn't untrue. I think I was trying to withhold myself from any gaze that felt like a demand. That felt like ownership. I didn't want to be made to explain this life to anyone who didn't already know it.

———

When I met my mother that first time, when I was in college, I had gone to Boston to attend a wedding. I have told this story: how I was staying at a suburban hotel and how in my mind my mother is standing at a distance, waiting. When I actually saw her, opening an apartment door, I was surprised that she and I were the same size, maybe because I hadn't thought to wonder about that before. I've told this story of our meeting, but what I haven't said is that I was in Boston with Evan and with Celia. The wedding we were attending was her niece's, and I was there as a mere guest of a guest, a plus-one.

The venue was a colonial-style estate, with paved paths, gardens, and wainscoting. Before the dinner, waiters circulated with hors d'oeuvres. A snow pea wrapped around the C of a shrimp tasted like it had been marinated in Wishbone Italian dressing, and for a long time after I would have sudden cravings for just that: cold shrimp, Wishbone, snow peas. I'd only been to weddings where food was served banquet-style, a bottle of cognac sat on every table, and the bride changed outfits two or three times.

It would have been impossible to conceal my meeting with my mother from Evan and Celia, so I didn't. Instead, I downplayed it. I pretended like it was just a quick visit to see her. My mind has elected to erase whether or not they asked questions, and what or how I responded, and what I kept to myself. Like maybe a lot of parent-child relationships, even metaphors or mimicries of one, mine and Celia's was part real, part play. As always, as in every relationship, I concealed more than I revealed. I was performing. I could be the audience, the actor, and all the in-betweens from the stage to the exit. I never again spoke of *Miss Saigon* to Evan or to Celia. I never told them how many nights I thought about its humiliations. They would reverberate across years of my life.

In Boston, my mother hadn't asked why I was there, finally meeting her. My dad had arranged it, as he would other visits. Maybe she thought I had come there just to see her. Or maybe she knew that I hadn't. This is who I was, always telling a slightly different story, depending on who was listening. Always I have somewhere else to be. A meeting, an obligation. I look ahead; I look at the time. My mother,

I think, agrees. She has never once urged me to stay. It feels like we are always ready to return to the lives we already have—I mean our regular lives, which do not include each other.

———

Evan and I broke up in college but stayed friends for a while, which meant I stayed in touch with Celia. But eventually all of that ended, too. A slow lessening on all sides. Evan and I didn't grow apart; we grew up. I deliberately do not write the details of our relationship because they aren't that interesting, not even to me. I think one of our last conversations was a dispute over a utility bill for a summer apartment we had shared. He claimed that he'd paid more and therefore that I owed him, which I didn't agree with, since I'd paid more of a different bill. He had always been rather cheap, which I considered inexcusable given how he had grown up, and I yelled at him for it.

In the decades that followed, I missed Celia the most. I would think of her whenever I used that monogrammed tote bag, or whenever I saw a 1960s picture of Jackie Kennedy. I would see horses in a distant field and think of Celia. But we had broken up, too, and I wasn't a person who kept in touch with exes. I went on, got married, and had two children. I heard through a friend from high school that

Evan did, too. I saw his name pop up on Facebook once, and ignored it. I didn't think Celia would be on social media, and she wasn't.

To friends, I've sometimes referred to Celia as the mother-in-law who got away. By that I mean a structure, a series of possibilities that can emerge from such a codified relationship. Because there's no one word for the kind of friendship Celia and I had, that I've never experienced since. In ways both gentle and blunt, Celia mentored and mothered me. She taught me ways of whiteness I couldn't have learned on my own. The hieroglyphics, as Wharton called them, of a coded society. I didn't know that then, but I know it now, in the same way I know that I must have been a lesson, a close study, in return.

After Evan and I broke up, before I lost touch with Celia entirely, I visited her and her husband in the small South Carolina town where they had moved for a while, for his work. They would end up moving again and again, and I had a sense that their marriage wouldn't last. Celia and I walked through the little downtown, and I got my first glimpses of Spanish moss draped over old trees, and serpentine stone walls that made me think of ghosts. We went into a card shop and idly I watched the woman behind the counter ring up purchases. In the background an eighties Elton John song was playing. Openly maudlin, not shy about synthesizers, the kind of song I associated with the dentist's office. *Some things look better*, he sings, *just passing through*. In this town in South Carolina, like so many places I'd been in my life up to that point, white people stared at me. Rarely did they bother to hide it. They seemed, instead, to stare hard on purpose. I should have been nervous or uncomfortable, as I usually was, but I wasn't. Because I was with Celia. A beautiful tall white woman who had grace in her stride and money in her purse. Her company, the clarity of being seen with her, was armor. Did she know this? What was I even doing there, visiting this woman to whom I had no logical claim? What did I think I deserved? It wasn't yet the last time I'd see Celia, but the moment held a strange sense of sorrow, the nostalgia that lasts the duration of an old pop song. I was already thinking ahead to the ending of it. What would play next. How, soon, I would leave this place and go back to college, back to whatever life I thought I was going to get to have after that.

9

THE STORY OF MY NAME

My mother, like everyone in my family, calls me by my given name: Bich. In Vietnam the name is quite ordinary, but in the conservative, mostly white town where I grew up girls had names like Jennifer, Amy, and Stacy. Bich (properly spelled *Bích* and pronounced "Bic," with an upward tonal accent, somewhere between a question and an exclamation) didn't just make me stand out; it made me miserably visible. Your name is what? people would say. How do you spell that? Sometimes they would laugh in my face. You know what your name looks like, right? Did your parents really name you that? They didn't know that for me, even the word *parents* was complicated, a designation that felt partly like a lie. They didn't know that every time I heard my name I felt a little jolt of shame and embarrassment—that feeling of being literally called out. I envied Vietnamese kids who had "good" easy names, like Linh and Vu. Like my sister's name, Anh. I wouldn't have changed those either. I also envied kids whose parents let them have separate "American" names. Phuoc at home could be Phil at school. But my dad and stepmom got angry at the very idea. I was not to be allowed to have a nickname, or use my middle name instead. My stepmom said that I had to be proud of who I was, and she wasn't wrong, but to me it was just another thing about my life that I had no say in. I was told—by my stepmom, by people throughout my life--that my name was my heritage, and that it would be a betrayal to change it. And so I stuck with Bich, or let it stick with me.

The last time I saw my mother, during the second summer of the pandemic, I asked what I had never thought to ask before: Why Bích? How did she choose that name?

That wasn't me, she said, in the matter-of-fact way that has become almost familiar, a characteristic I know about my mother. It was your grandma, your ba noi.

I must have looked surprised, because she laughed a little. Your ba noi wanted to decide and I figure, What is it to me? Let her choose. Just a name.

My mother and I never talk about how I grew up. As far as she is concerned, my sister and I were fine and cared for, and the proof is that we are here. I would never tell her that some of my earliest memories of school include the fear of roll call, me trying to volunteer my name before the teacher could attempt a pronunciation. The kindest teachers were the ones who asked me directly how to say it. In classes of almost all white kids, it wasn't difficult to figure out who would have my name. But mostly, teachers would call out "Beech" or "Beesh," or they'd preface it with, I'm going to butcher this. Beech Nugent? I recently read a study about the lasting harm and internalized racism that can result when kids consistently hear their names being mispronounced in the classroom. I know that I'm still dealing with that harm. I was a short, shy child with heavy glasses, and my name made me even shyer. I learned that if I avoided meeting people I could avoid having to say and thus repeat and explain my name. This became a habit that continued well into adulthood. I didn't realize that I was also taking on the shame of not being strong enough to handle the shame of the American gaze.

The word *bích* refers to a kind of jade. Growing up, I knew that every Vietnamese girl was supposed to wear a jade bracelet, growing into it so that the bracelet would become impossible to remove except by breakage. The stone was meant to protect, to heal, even if it did feel like entrapment. And the greener the jade, the better. In a different country, in a different life, my given name would be just as beautiful, just as complex.

For a couple of years, around middle school, I wore a green jade bracelet because my grandmother had always worn one. To this day, my mother wears one, too. I saw it as a private point of Vietnameseness that might seem, to anyone who didn't know, like just a piece of jewelry. But the jade would clang against counters, desks. I bumped myself in the head with it so many times, washing my hair, turning in my sleep. One day, when I just couldn't bear it anymore, I dipped my arm in a sink full of warm, soapy water and forced the bracelet off. It had been hard to put on in the first place and I guessed that I must have grown a little, after all, because it hurt so much I thought I might damage a bone. But then I felt the give. The bracelet, free of me, became a piece of jade that I would never know what to do with again.

———

Names, like everything in this country, reveal our relationships with race and racism. For so many people of color, the implications can be deeply layered and far-reaching. I can only speak, here, to my own experiences. Because names are both deeply personal and deeply public. We have to see our names all the time. Every form, every email. *Your name here* at the top of every assignment in elementary school. Other kids would decorate their names with stars and hearts, because the sight of their names gave them pleasure and satisfaction. Like wearing a necklace that spells out your own name. Like people in the eighties who spent so many hours at the video arcade because they were determined to have their name listed on the top score Galactica screen. I have never accessed this desire, this pride, this sense of claim. It was not a thrill to see my name on the bulletin board when I won the elementary school spelling bee. Years later, it was not the thrill I thought it was supposed to be to see my name in print. Sometimes I think about how this has hindered my writing life, or my publishing life anyway. It has made me hesitant, self-sabotaging, filled with regret. After my first book was published under my given name, I was told that my name was cemented. Once, at a literary party in New York, a thing and a place that were not part of my normal life, I overheard another writer laughing at my name. She didn't know I was standing right there, listening as she said to someone else, Can you believe anyone would have a name like that? I wonder what she would think if she knew that my reaction was not horror, not anger, but the thrill of righteous shame. That feeling of *I knew it. I knew that's what people really thought.* When my second book was published, it was reviewed in *The New York Times* along with a couple of other books under the subheading "International." My book was not international. It was a novel set in the American Midwest. The most international-seeming thing about the book was the author's name: Bich Minh Nguyen.

The perception of Nguyen, though, has shifted. Because it's by far the most common Vietnamese surname, and apparently now the thirty-eighth most common surname in the United States, it has gone from seeming foreign and unpronounceable to acceptably different and only somewhat unpronounceable. The first time a TSA agent said, Have a good flight, Ms. Nguyen, and got it as correct as any American can, I felt what can only be described as triumph: we were so many, we could not be ignored. I'm still waiting for this turn, this kind of approval, for Bich and, yes, hating myself for wanting it.

Wherever I go, I'm quietly studying people's names—the cadences, spellings, and sounds. I listen to pronunciation guides. I keep track of the Social Security Administration's compilations of the most popular baby names, listed by year and by decade. I keep track of writers and celebrities who have changed their names. I keep track, too, of seemingly safe names that suddenly turned. I take no pleasure at the morphing of Karen, not even if there are Karens who once laughed at me; they now have to live with some of the discomfort I have always known.

Just a name, my mother said, as so many people have. Then why does it seem so fraught to change it? How do we decide which meaning, and whose symbolism, and whose social and cultural pressures to follow? In the United States, more than seventy percent of women change their last name when they get married. My stepmom didn't, and neither did I. But everyone seems to have an opinion no matter what.

———

The thing about names is that they are markers of respect. What we call someone, what we are allowed to call someone, what we insist on calling someone—all of these indicate relationships having to do with levels of understanding, familiarity, or power. How many people go by nicknames that were fixed by others, that they maybe don't even like but feel it's easier to keep using? How many people have acquiesced to going by initials or shortened versions of their names because English-speaking people told them they would never be able to pronounce their whole "foreign" names? How many trans people have encountered people who refuse to acknowledge their chosen names? How many people keep or take a name out of pure obligation?

For most of my life, I tried to inhabit the name that my

grandmother gave me. Sometimes I wrote it out with the accent, to emphasize that it was not an American word. But I could never get away from having to explain it, which always felt like explaining my very self, justifying myself. In truth, most of the people who claimed to like the name Bich, or who expressed outrage and horror at the idea of my changing it, have been white. They told me the name was cool, was interesting, was unique, was being true to myself, was an important part of my cultural identity. They said it would break their hearts if I changed my name. They did not say they wished to have the name themselves. I wanted to believe them; for a long time, I made a choice to believe them. But I knew, too, that they liked the exotic so long as they didn't have to live with it. They liked the idea of the exotic, not thinking about how *exotic* might benefit the person deciding what exotic is. Sometimes I wondered if they also liked feeling bad for me. It is one of my historical facts that the name Bich is steeped in shame because living in the United States as a refugee and a child of refugees was steeped in shame. America made sure I knew that anxiety from my earliest moments of awareness. I cannot detach the name Bich from my childhood, cannot detach it from the experience of people laughing at me, calling me a bitch, letting me know that I'm the punch line of my own joke, too stupid or afraid to do anything but take it. When I see the letters that spell out that name, I see a version of self I've had to create, to hide. Even now, typing the letters, I want to turn away. America has ruined the name Bich for me, and I have let it.

I can't write about my name without writing about racism, and I can't write about racism without writing about anti-Asian violence, which has risen sharply during the pandemic. I had overheard my dad and uncles whispering about the murder of Vincent Chin in Detroit, in 1982. The two white guys who beat him to death—one was overheard saying, "It's because of you little motherfuckers that we're out of work"—got probation and a $3,000 fine. A civil suit later awarded his family $1.5 million that they never received.

So, I've always told myself, It could be much worse. At least you're okay. At least you're still here. I am well trained, self-trained, in being grateful for whatever I get to have. Anyone whose family has emerged from long histories of imperialism and colonization, I think, contends with this. The violence that is internal and internalized won't kill, at least not directly. And because America has always told me that I'm overreacting. Because look at the model minority myth. Because crazy rich Asians (because all Asians are alike). Because it's not meant to be malicious, laughing at Asian names or accents. It's not a big deal. I know, because it keeps happening, in media and in real life. And when we express anger about it we are countered with, you're too sensitive; it's just a joke. I get it—the joke is more important than our existence.

———

I confess: there were years I forgot my mother's full name. After that first visit in Boston, I wrote her name and phone number in a notebook that I soon lost. I had to ask my dad how to contact her for the next visit, between college and grad school. He was the person who kept track of her phone numbers, which would change when she moved apartments. Once, I called an old number and got a pastry shop. Though she refers to herself as Mommy, I have managed to avoid calling her by any name. Hi, Bich, hi honey, she says, the few times she has called me. It's your mommy. Hi, I say. How are you?

———

In childhood, with all the hours of television I watched, I would try out different names in my head, pretending to be Samantha, Blair, Alyssa, Heather, Ashley. But I was realistic: they were too pretty-girl for the likes of me. I couldn't pull off a dramatic name like Vivian and Anastasia either. How about Beatrice? I once asked a friend. She laughed and said, never.

I was in my thirties, in that stretch of years when I wasn't in communication with my mother, when I became Beth, a simple, ordinary name that had been there all along. By then I had a toddler and a baby, both of whom thought my name was Mama. I was still having to repeat and explain the name Bich to everyone I met, and deal with the comments and jokes, feeling like I had no choice but to endure. And then one day I realized that I would have to repeat and explain to my kids' teachers, too, and to other parents. "What are your parents' or guardians' names?" It would go on and on. And maybe one day my kids would feel the secret shame that I knew so well, but secondhand—an embarrassment about their mother.

I had always given fake names at restaurants, often borrowing Rose or Sophia from *The Golden Girls*. The summer I became Beth, the kids and I were in New York, and one day I went over to Shake Shack in Madison Square Park. A woman behind the counter took my order and asked the dreaded question of what my name was, and I said, Beth. She nodded. She did not doubt my answer. And in that moment, it felt real: I wasn't just saying Beth; I *was* Beth. So I started to say it more. To salespeople. To babysitters, electricians, new acquaintances, new colleagues. I'd say Beth, and a tiny blast of joy, like cool air from the refrigerator on a hot day, would come over me. Like a secret self. Like another life.

Beth is a social experiment, a hypothesis that life in

America is easier with a quiet name that no one ever gets wrong. And it's true. I am seen as less Asian and more American with the name Beth. Experiencing that difference, glimpsing a bit of that yellow peril, has been instant, insightful, painful. As Bich, I am a foreigner who makes people a little uncomfortable. As Beth, I am never complimented on my English.

My closest friends accepted this name right away. Others expressed surprise, disapproval. A number of people informed me that they would continue to call me by my given name no matter what. What felt like freedom to me was viewed by some as the kind of cultural betrayal they'd warned me against, as if it were my duty to bear what they did not. But here is the thing: I am not Beth to make life easier for everyone else; I am Beth to make life easier for me.

Is changing my name strategic, safe, self-care, selling out? I've been trying to figure this out, trying to write this down, for years. I love that people are now talking about how important it is to learn name pronunciations. But a tiny part of me also feels a sorrowful sense of, damn. Because, like so many recognitions, it arrived too late for my generation. Because being Bich, and growing up as Bich in a mostly white town in the eighties, felt like a test that I was constantly failing. It was a double bind: the people who made me uncomfortable with my given name also thought that I'd be betraying my heritage by changing it. I don't mean only white people. A lot of people of color have wanted me to know that they're proud to have kept their names instead of choosing something easy. That they have the strength and courage that I have lacked.

What I have always wanted was to be nameless, free from the gaze. But because that is impossible, I am instead always betraying somebody.

Still, because I haven't gone to the trouble of legally changing my name, I am Bich on all of my documents. My kids know my given name, and it's startling to me how normal they think it is to have two names, getting to choose which to use at what time. That's a measure of progress, at least. But a while back, at a store with my older son, I had to show my driver's license and the woman checking it started laughing. Is that really your name? she asked, a question I've gotten a lot and that has always perplexed me. I think a former self would have gone along with the laughter to avoid discomfort. I am so used to apologizing, saying, Yeah, it's a weird or tricky or difficult name. But my child was with me, so instead I stared back at the woman until she was the one who was uncomfortable. As we left, he said to me, That lady was making fun of your name. That's mean. It was the first time, maybe, he had witnessed this. He and his brother are both Vietnamese and white. They have simple, straightforward first names that, in America, no one ever mispronounces. But sometimes a stranger will ask me, in a voice of disapproval, why I didn't give them traditional Vietnamese names. I can't help hearing that as yet another demand to justify my cultural existence.

A while back, my kids were learning about the origin of languages. They were curious about how words and sounds evolve, which I'm always trying to understand, too. One of my kids said, Did people who spoke in Middle English know it was Middle English? We talked about how sometimes a word, like *cleave*, becomes its own opposite, both definitions retaining usable meaning. Maybe we are all trying to understand the loss of a language as it turns into something else. Is it always a loss? Or does it always feel that way? I tell my kids that sometimes the shifts are so slow that they're recognized only a tiny bit at a time. That language changes all around us, and we are part of it. Like slang, like idioms, new words, new pronunciations. Words don't shift on their own. We must do the shifting. Sometimes we, too, are our own opposites.

The last time I saw my mother in Boston, when she told me that my grandmother Noi had been the one to choose my name, I did not tell her that I was going by Beth now. I wasn't worried about her reaction, and I realized that maybe I knew her enough to predict that she wouldn't have cared at all. I was held back by my internal uncertainty about what it meant to go against my grandmother, who had made so much of my life possible.

As a Gen X woman of color, I grew up hating myself because that's what we did back then. Now both therapy and pop culture say I'm supposed to love myself, take care of myself. But instead, I fall back on what I know. I sit around, feeling anxious. I let piles of paper and books accumulate, listening to songs that hurt me. I let the worst memories keep me awake at night. I go over so many things I said, or never said, and achieve no resolution. It has taken the writing of this to realize how much time I have let go by, how much of my life has been absolutely ruled by fear. Is it really possible that my mother has hugged me hello and good-bye but that I have never truly held her? That I never thought about this until now? I'm still trying to figure out how to react to the strangeness that is my own story, my own names. That, too, is part of refugeetude. We do not outrun our origins. If we don't contend, they will contend with us.

So when I say that right now Beth is where I have shifted, I also mean that it does not change my past, my family, our lives as refugees in the United States. This name may not be forever. It just feels like a bit of space, where I can direct how I am seen rather than be directed. I realize that, my whole life, I have been waiting for some kind of permission—my own permission—to be here.

10

APPARENT, REVISITED

Half a year into the pandemic, I called my mother in Boston.
By then, most restaurants, casinos, and grocery stores, places
she might have gone, were temporarily closed or restricted,
and I pictured her waiting it out in her apartment. I figured
she was fine because I would have heard otherwise from my
dad. This is the system my sister and I still rely on, one of
the forms of communication that take place in the shadows
and backgrounds of our lives.

My mother answered the phone right away. I've been
home all this time, she said. Don't go anywhere. Scared to
go anywhere. She turned the questions on me: Was I being
careful? Was I working?

The two boys, she said, because that's how she refers to

my kids, maybe forgetting their names. Are the two boys okay?

It was the first September of the pandemic, and everyone in my house had gone back to school and work by looking at screens. We had moved from California to Wisconsin the year before, and hadn't had much time to establish close friendships. We would spend many months sitting and teaching and learning in different rooms with our different computers, trying to pay attention. I knew we were lucky to have this, to have work and space. I felt almost strangely prepared, partly because the Midwest was my most familiar landscape, and because my whole life I'd been a homebody, consciously grateful for shelter, for electricity, for washing machines, for running water that arrives at the turn of a handle. I had always stocked up on groceries and medicine. Not hoarding, just gathering what might be needed in case of emergency, in the same way I kept a go bag under my bed, and never walked into a building without looking for the exits.

Over the phone, my mother assured me she was fine. In fact, she had nothing to do. She just sat around at home. I assured her I was fine, too. It was a brief, two-minute call. There was nothing left to tell, so we said good-bye.

———

The following March, a white man murdered eight people, six of whom were Asian women, at three spas in metro Atlanta. Anti-Asian hate crimes had been increasing steadily for well over a year, fueled by politicians who called COVID the Chinese flu. My Asian friends and I texted each other often, sharing our worries. Elders were being shoved on the street; Asians were being punched and attacked on sidewalks and subways. And then the Atlanta shootings.

When I was a kid, racism against Asians was so commonplace, such a regular part of life—making fun of what and how we ate; commenting that "the Japanese" were going to take over everything—that we didn't even call it racist. In Michigan, the auto industry used to depict Toyota and Honda as anti-American, and it was said that anyone who drove such a car near Detroit would risk being keyed, or worse. I didn't doubt it, because of Vincent Chin.

I called my mother in Boston again.

Jesus Christ, she said. Everything is so bad out there.

I asked how often she went outside, and did she go by herself?

She gave a little laugh. I don't go nowhere. Jesus Christ, she said again. It was a verbal tic she'd picked up, I couldn't recall when.

We talked about the vaccines and it turned out that we had gotten our first doses within days of each other.

Even over the phone, conversation with her was like being in a very small room, an attic space with just one stipple of a window. It was like playing hide-and-seek so well that no one would ever find us. I thought about faraway words like *race*, *identity*, *justice*—words she and I had never exchanged. How I was well past graduate school when I learned the term *code-switching*, though I'd been doing it my whole life, switching from group to group, switching even within groups, and within my own family. How rarely it occurred to me to wonder who else was doing the same. Including my mother in Boston, switching into English, switching into whoever she was when she spoke to me.

I called her again after the second dose of the vaccine. A couple of weeks after that, I called her again. And then again. I'd never talked to her so much in my life. Was it the pandemic? Was it the simple fact that calling more led to calling more? Had it been just this easy the whole time?

We never stayed on the phone longer than a few minutes. She asked the same questions each time: where were my kids and was I working. She always asked about work but never asked what it involved. Maybe work was just work and the most important thing about it was that it was happening. I asked the same things, too: how her other kids were doing, how her family in Vietnam was doing, what she did all day.

I spent a lot of time at my desk, which sat at an upstairs

window that had a view of neighbors' backyards. All winter I had stared out at a tangle of leafless branches and snow-patched ground. One of the neighbors had painted the door of their gray-shingled shed a bright yellow and my eye would go right to it. Sometimes it seemed like the only spot of color out there in days of cloud cover.

Then one day I saw a pop of green leaves; another day, pink flowers. I started to hear the mourning doves again, those birds that speak their desolation so insistently. For me, they are connected to the feeling of summer—how slowly it begins, how quickly it all ends, and how I first felt this when I was a little girl sitting on my next-door neighbor's back porch when they were away. A few moments of stolen solitude in a place I wasn't supposed to be. And those loud, sad birds calling out from wherever they were in the trees.

Sometimes I would ask my mother how things were going and she would answer by saying, Jesus Christ. It was not an admonishment, not anger or frustration. More like a semicolon, an em dash. One day I asked her again how she and my dad had met. I wanted to know how they had stayed together long enough to have two kids, and what had their relationship been like? She had never really answered before. But this time, she laughed.

Oh my god, she said, and if it is possible for a voice to sound like years going by, hers was it.

I thought of the black-and-white photo of her that I found in my dad and stepmom's house. That photo of my dad as a young man, leaning against his motorbike. I had never before connected the two images in my mind: separate, but nearly touching.

I got a letter from him one day in Vietnam, my mother said. He said he's going to marry someone. He needed someone to take care of you girls. And him, she added, with a little laugh.

I looked out the window. I listened to my mother. We had more time than we'd ever had, and nowhere to go.

———

But then, in late spring: possibilities. A writing residency I'd been awarded a year and a half earlier was now resuming, with pandemic precautions. I could go there, to upstate New York in the summer, and stop in Boston along the way. As with every visit to see my mother, I would have another plan, another event surrounding it. Another reason for being there and another reason for leaving.

I called my sister to ask her to come to Boston, too. I said we could meet at O'Hare and fly to Logan together, as we had that time she had looked out the window and been seized with a fear that we were going to fall into the water. I pictured us walking around Boston with our kids. We could stay in the same hotel, have coffee at outdoor cafes, and go, together, to see our mother. If the kids couldn't go, because the vaccine for my youngest wasn't available yet, then maybe it could be just us. We could eat wherever we wanted without having to figure out kid preferences, and take a long weekend away. I could already see us taking selfies with our mother. I could see us agreeing, later, in a cab, that we didn't understand how she lived, how she spent her hours. We would go to museums and walk around, together, in our masks, determined to be tourists and not just daughters.

At first, Anh agreed. Then, a couple of weeks later, she said, I'm not sure. She said the calendar wasn't looking so good. She said she had a lot of work, and maybe we could go later in the year?

In the end, I went to Boston by myself. I blamed the various logistics of life and work, sure. But the reality is probably as simple as it ever was, said without judgment: I was the one who wanted to go and could go, at the same time. Slowly, I was understanding that it was not for me to make someone else—not even my sister, the only person who shares the same mother—take part in my narrative.

———

The day before I visited my mother, I went to the Institute of Contemporary Art with an old friend who had driven in from a suburb. We wandered into a giant installation that I had encountered a few years before in a different museum: Ragnar Kjartansson's *The Visitors*, an hour-long collaborative video projected onto nine enormous screens, each showing different musicians in separate rooms of the same giant old house, performing the same song at the same time. I remembered the song, its repeated refrains, how it builds a melancholy that becomes exultation. It's impossible to see every screen, every view, at once, and so you end up walking around the dark vast room. Eventually, my friend and I sat on the floor, as everyone does when they commit to a view, to follow the song's progress. On the screens, the musicians begin to gather, leaving their separate scenes and instruments and merging toward one camera. Someone opens a bottle of champagne. They keep the music with them, singing. They go outside, beyond the porch where others are hanging out, and drift toward a deep green meadow and a farther off body of water. They keep singing, a ragtag parade. It's impossible not to want to go with them, to go with the song. But the camera doesn't. It stays as the players move farther away, taking the sound with them. It has to let them disappear.

I kept thinking about my kids, who had seen *The Visitors*, too, years earlier when we were in San Francisco. We had sat together to finish the song. I was, all these months into the pandemic that was not over, having a hard time being away from them. I had never left them for longer than a week, and now it would be almost a month. Every now and then I'd feel a prickle of panic as if I'd forgotten to pick them up from school. Once, pregnant with my second child, I'd had this very moment of panic while at a playground: there was one child, but where was the other one? I'd had to remember that he was still inside my body.

Does every parent live with a kind of permanent separation anxiety that only sleep or denial can allay? It feels for me like a condition of motherhood. It makes me rethink my own childhood all the time, as if I'll be able to understand it better from this different lens. The turn from child to adult still feels sudden, a snap of the fingers under my nose. Like when I first read Beverly Cleary's Ramona books to my children and realized that I had crossed over from identifying with Ramona to identifying with her mother. For me, motherhood, like being a refugee, has meant being in multiple consciousnesses at the same time, and never feeling sure about any of them.

———

It rained that time I brought my kids to see my mother in Boston. Four years later, it was raining again when a cab dropped me off at her apartment complex. I called her from the parking lot, as she had instructed, as I had every time I'd come to visit her, so she could come out to meet me.

When my mother appeared in the doorway of her building, she was masked but instantly knowable. By now, I think I would recognize her even out of the context of this place, which is almost the only place I have ever seen her. I recognize her body in a way that is like recognizing my own in a reflective window. It's always a little startling. My mother looks delicate, but she isn't delicate. She takes purposeful steps.

Where are the two boys? she called out.

Remember? I said. They couldn't travel after all.

I couldn't tell if she had forgotten or if she hadn't believed me in the first place.

Up close she took hold of my upper arm like she was going to yank me off a stage, and we walked like that to the door of her building.

The last time I was in her apartment there had been a collection of things like napkins, tea, toiletries, and water bottles arranged on a sheet on the floor. Now a small dining table took their place. A floral-print curtain covered the broken window blinds, and a pink blanket covered the sofa, a bed pillow propped up at one end. I felt certain that she or her husband slept there often, to nap or to call it a night.

My mother's husband—improbably, it seemed to me,

my stepfather—lifted his hand in a cheerful hello. He was sitting at the table, watching a movie on his phone. I could hear dialogue in Chinese, and the familiar sounds of gunfire, crashes, and explosions.

My mother made me take the other chair at the table while she perched on a shorter wooden stool. We argued briefly about who should sit on the more comfortable chair, until her husband stood up and offered his. My mother waved her hand at us both, definitively, and sat on the stool.

She asked the same questions. How are the boys? I showed her pictures on my phone and she praised them. Two boys, she repeated with approval.

I complimented her outfit: a light silken jacket the color of crimson pluots, a jumpsuit printed with abstract panda bears, a knit cap covering her head.

She had also rearranged the altar, and I noticed a picture of a good-looking young man with fine cheekbones, wearing an army uniform, next to the framed photos of her parents—my maternal grandparents.

My mother said, That's my brother.

I'd forgotten about her siblings: one brother, two sisters.

Her brother had died in the war when he was thirty-one. He had no family, my mother said, shaking her head. No kids. No wife. Not even a girlfriend!

Her two sisters were still in Saigon, also in their seventies.

It's so bad now in Vietnam, my mother said. She meant COVID, which had been kept at bay but was starting to ravage, with not enough vaccines available. My mother had been going to Vietnam almost every year, and she was impatient to see her sisters again. She didn't know when she'd get the next chance.

It's funny, she said suddenly, I dream about my brother all the time.

He visits you? I asked. I don't know why I said it that way; the words took shape as I spoke them.

Yes. She nodded, agreeing with that description, smiling when she looked over at him again. He visits me.

I'm getting so old, she went on. I know I still look pretty good. Much better than most Americans my age. But still. I'm old, you know.

Her father had died when he was around age sixty-seven, she said. Some kind of cancer, maybe. No one really knew. But her mother had lived to ninety-something. Remember? she said, because she had mentioned this to me before. I did remember. It was one of those facts I wanted to hang on to, for the sense of hope it contained.

The whole time we were talking, her husband stared at his phone. Our conversation was punctuated by the sounds of street fights, the acting noises of wounds and wounding that were so familiar from my childhood.

My mother and I walked around the apartment together, looking at the old photos she had up. Most were faded from years of daylight. There was an 8 x 10 of herself, framed and glassed, smooth-skinned at age fifty.

See how good I look? she said.

I stopped at the older pictures of her daughter and son, and more recent pictures of her grandchildren. My niece and nephew, grown-up. One still lived nearby; the other was now living in a different state.

There was a picture of my sister and me, taken on the day of my sister's wedding, she in a white gown and me in a bridesmaid dress. I had seen this picture before but hadn't fully registered the strangeness of my mother having a portrait from a wedding to which she hadn't even been invited. Of course, my dad must have sent it years ago. My sister didn't send photos and neither did I.

A small analog clock hung on one wall—a real clock, as my kids call it—and I couldn't stop glancing at it. How long would this visit last? How long had any of my visits lasted? When in our lifetimes would we cross the twenty-four-hour mark, and how many visits would it take? Over the phone, I'd asked my mother if she wanted to get some lunch. Or maybe go for a walk around the neighborhood? We can go anywhere you want, I said, instantly regretting how it sounded. Like I was trying to be so generous. I eat at home, she had said, matter-of-factly, and she repeated it when I was in her apartment. You want something to eat? You want something to drink? I declined, as I think by now she knew I would.

She said that her son, my half brother, wanted her to move in with him and his wife, in their house that was about thirty minutes away. They'd been asking for years. It's a nice, good house, my mother said. It's big, too. But I don't want to go there. She also had the option to live with her daughter and son-in-law, who had moved farther away, but she didn't want to go there either.

I asked why not.

She waved her hand, a gesture of dismissal. Why I want to live with other people? They always ask me so many questions. I want to be myself, in my own place.

I looked over at her husband, who was still staring at his phone, at his movie, and my mother gave a little laugh. He doesn't care, she said. He didn't even look up at us.

I felt a sense of time falling into itself—geographies bending—my mother and her husband in Boston suddenly seeming like my stepmom and my dad in Michigan. Their lives had gone in nearly opposite directions, but now, in their seventies, they all wanted to be at home, to be on their own, even to be left alone. How they'd all chosen to stay in places they didn't love because it was too hard and too much effort to do otherwise. Eventually, the displacement becomes the home. Eventually, time becomes inertia, or maybe it's the other way around.

It was peaceful here, in my mother's place, in a way I had never perceived it to be before. It felt tucked back from the rest of the outside world. So it was, too, in that cottage-like house in Michigan. When the television wasn't on and music wasn't playing, I could hear the same birds of my youth, whose noises and names I had mostly never learned. I could hear the scrape and thud of distant machinery, building over spaces that had once been woods.

I asked my mother if she had slept next to me and my sister, when we were babies. I asked about my name. I asked her the same questions I'd asked before—where and when I was born, where and when my sister was born. I wanted, after all this time, a remembered detail. A hospital? A street? Who had helped her?

She said of course she had slept next to us. She said, Your ba noi chose your name. She made all the decisions and I say, Let her.

My mother laughed a small, kind laugh. She's a great lady, your ba noi.

I mentioned what she had told me over the phone, that

my dad had sent a letter to her in Vietnam all those years ago, telling her that he was getting married. I wondered why he had done that.

Oh, my mother said, her voice indicating that the answer was so obvious. He wanted me to know that you and Anh were okay because you had a new mommy.

Oh, I said.

I was so glad, my mother added. She's a very nice lady, and I'm glad.

What else do you remember? I asked.

I wanted to know what might be mine to know about my dad and my mother's relationship—how it had come to be, how it had come to not be. My mother had always talked about that day in 1975 when she realized that the rest of us had fled the country, and how she had cried. But I wanted to know what she felt after that, as the years went on, and years later when she came to the United States. Had she wanted to see us in Michigan? Had she tried? Had she been patiently waiting for an invitation? What were all the decisions that the adults had made, that my sister and I never knew about? My dad had never encouraged us to keep up with our Vietnamese, never lamented the way it seeped away from us, and I suddenly wondered if maybe it was even a secret relief, at times. The way he and his brothers and his friends could speak in Vietnamese right in front of us, confident that we would only partly, and then barely, understand what he was saying.

I asked my mother what else she could tell me. About the long past. About our origins. What had she been like, as a young woman? What had my dad been like? What lives might my sister and I have had, if we had never left Vietnam? What had she wanted? What had she settled for?

And my mother answered.

———

More than an hour later, which felt like some kind of record, my sixth visit with my mother was over. We had said as much as would be said and now were just looking at each other, casting around the room again, taking pictures that I would keep to myself.

I said good-bye to her husband, and he glanced up from his phone and waved. My mother and I put our shoes back on and walked into the hall and down the stairwell. I never saw anyone else in the stairwells of the buildings she'd lived in.

We crossed the parking lot together, toward the street where a car was supposed to meet me. My mother wondered out loud if it would rain again, and we both looked up at the clouds as if they would tell us.

Do you take a lot of walks? I asked.

I do take walks, she said, like she was conceding something. I go by myself. I had some good friends—she gestured at the apartments—but they all died.

I'm so sorry, I said, but my mother shrugged.

They got sick and they got old. That's what happens.

I could see a car turning onto the street, easing toward the curb. My mother and I walked toward it. I waved to the driver.

You go to New York now? my mother said. I had told her, earlier, that I would be heading upstate.

Be careful, she said.

You too, I said.

However we meant it—physically, bodily, the pandemic, the mind—we said what surely every mother says a hundred thousand times in a life. As safeguard, as superstition. *Be careful.* I keep forgetting, or rather keep having to remind myself, that my mother and I were, are, both mothers.

Maybe because *mother* is a word that, for us, keeps shifting. When I was growing up, I never said *mother* out loud in Vietnamese, though I had observed the word being used in other Vietnamese households, when my dad would bring us kids to parties. How would one speak the sound of *mother*, and what would that feel like? I wouldn't know, wouldn't say the word in a sentence, until I was in college, taking

Vietnamese-language classes. I have never, not even once, not even now, called my mother by her Vietnamese names.

———

At the end of that summer, after I saw my mother in Boston, after the writing residency, I drove to Michigan. Only my older son joined me, because the vaccine wasn't yet available for my younger son's age group. The car ride took nearly six hours from our home in Wisconsin, rounding Chicago toward the giant *Welcome to Pure Michigan* billboards. We would stay five or six days in a hotel and gather at my dad and stepmom's house with my siblings and cousins, uncles and aunts, almost all of them traveling in from other parts of the country. We had stacks of masks and antigen tests ready for this family reunion.

For years, my dad and stepmom have talked about selling their cottage house and moving away from Grand Rapids. The problem is, they don't know where to go. And it's hard to imagine. My dad has grown into this city and the city has grown around him. The Vietnamese population has expanded into the thousands since we landed there in 1975, and it is by far the place where my dad has lived the longest. It's where he met his Saigon Market friends, as we always called them, even though he's moved on now, and where he still attends and sometimes hosts Vietnamese parties that, to this day, I associate with crooning voices, disco balls, Hennessy X.O, silver trays piled with cha gio, and the sight of people dancing the cha-cha-cha.

Before my family gathered, I took my son to see Florence Street. My sister and her husband and now-teenage kid joined us, though only Anh and I could possibly have been interested in our old neighborhood of treeless sidewalks and 1950s houses, where mid-century did not mean modern. We might have been anywhere in Michigan, on any residential street on a Friday morning where no one is home because they're all at work. But our home happened to be here; we happened to have ended up in this half-brick, half-olive-siding ranch house with a living room picture window.

A few years before we moved away, my dad and stepmom financed an addition to the back of the house to create a dining room and a walk-out family room off the basement. Because the house had been built into a hillside, the new dining room felt almost like being on a real second-story level. It even had a windowed, salmon-colored side door that would, one day, open to a deck that my dad swore he would build. It would be perfect for summer, and grilling, and hanging out, and it would have a staircase that he would build, too, leading down to the backyard. My siblings and I were forbidden from touching that door, since it opened to a sheer drop to the ground. But we did anyway, of course, because it was there and we could not resist feeling, over and over, what it was like to open a door to nothing. Like a fantastical scene from a movie, like a bad dream, like an outtake from one of the MTV videos we loved. Eventually, my dad removed the doorknob so we couldn't mess around with it anymore. In its place he stuffed a wad of paper towel that stayed through winter and rain, on through the rest of the time that we lived in that house.

You would think I would've been embarrassed by that bright door cut into the house, and sometimes I was, but mostly it was delightfully comical, Seussian, and the kids in the neighborhood thought it was neat. I would see the door whenever I walked home from school. I would glance at it when playing outside. It was a glaring reminder of what it was to wait, to be filled with expectation. The door to nowhere is what my siblings and I called it. After we moved and got old enough to drive ourselves, we would go past the house every few years, to see if the people who lived there had added a deck. But through high school and beyond college, the house stayed as it was.

Anh and I couldn't remember the last time we had stopped by Florence Street. Had someone ever added a deck?

The trees in the yard had grown so much that they hid

the once-open view to the side of the house. We had to step closer to see: a weathered wooden deck bearing a grill, table, chairs. The salmon-colored door had been replaced, but the promise, at least, had been fulfilled.

It looked much closer to the ground than we remembered, the same way that everything from our childhood now seemed out of proportion, smaller, skewed by our own aging.

My sister's husband suggested that we ask the owners if we could look inside. No way, Anh and I said in unison. He laughed in his easygoing way and went right up to the front door and rang the bell. He peered through the picture window, the one I had spent so much time staring out of when I was a kid, ducking if I saw a car coming down the street. No one was home. Months later, I would search for photos on real estate sites and find empty rooms where my dad's original tile and carpet still lay. I would recognize the brass lighting fixture he and my stepmom had chosen for the dining room. But more recent pictures showed all of it gone—the dining room turned into a bedroom, every inch of flooring replaced by engineered hardwood.

Standing in front of that house, I turned around to face the sloping street that ended right at the yard we had called ours. I had so many nightmares of cars flying down and crashing into us. Sometimes the headlights of a car at night did shine right into the living room, tracking a left or right turn along the walls, but the neighborhood didn't then, and didn't now, get much traffic. It was still mostly quiet, mostly empty, working class mixing with the middle.

This is where we rode our bikes all summer long, Anh and I told our children, who were gentle with their disinterest. We pointed out the houses of the neighbors we remembered, naming them. Did they still live there?

Do you remember how you had a crush on Jonathan up the street? Remember the Johnsons' white cat that had one blue eye and one green eye? Whatever happened to the Morrow sisters, who were so odd and so sad?

My best frenemy had lived in a white house next to ours, with a yard that was ChemLawn green and obsessively mowed. Her mother had lined their hallways with plastic runners as a shield against childhood mess. Her father had power-washed the garage door. Whoever owned the house now had no such concerns. They had built a clumsy portico over the front door, let weeds overtake the former garden and push into fractures in the driveway.

What had happened to my old frenemy, to the people of our childhood? Did they come back to this place, too, their own years distorting what they thought they knew for sure about the past?

We drove the few blocks to the elementary school where Anh and I had taken Drownproofing lessons. The playground had that summertime look of an abandoned park, but I supposed that everyone's childhood playgrounds looked haunted in some way. It's just that we are the ones doing the haunting.

My son retrieved a basketball from the car and played with his cousin and uncle while Anh and I watched from a swing set. We were busy remembering all the lost things, all the gone things. The wooden teeter-totters. The high metal slides. Hanging on to the merry-go-round so as not to get flung off. Those odd wooden squares with springs underneath them, where you could bounce someone off if they were standing diagonally from you. Do you remember that concrete wading pool? The yards we cut through, dark winter mornings, to get to school faster?

Before getting back in the car, we all walked over to the nature trail that ran behind the school. It followed a familiar creek, still the same brown of watered-down chocolate milk. Look, I said, pointing at a rope swing tied to a tree branch. There had been one decades ago, too, and intrepid older kids would try to make it to the other bank or deliberately splash into the water. Anh and I had never tried. Never would. Later I would ask my son what he thought of the spaces of my childhood and he would say, No offense, but it was kind of sad and depressing. One day, he said, am I going to do this same thing and go visit the schools I went to in California before we moved and it will be kind of sad and depressing?

I'd forgotten, in the minutiae of my own childhood, that my children would have their own to attend to. It made me want to cry as we drove toward my parents' house. 28th Street. Kalamazoo Street. East Paris. The Beltline. The aggravating divided highways where left turns can only be done by U-turns, known as Michigan Lefts. I didn't know that getting older would feel like this, time's sorrow making every farewell a harder one. Even in places that I had wanted to get away from.

I write what I don't know how to say out loud, which is that being in the city where I grew up makes me feel that particular, long-ago feeling of summer as silence, when freedom from school was also the bittersweetness of change. A couple of kids would move away, and I would never find out why or what happened to them. I'll never know how their lives turned out. There was a boy named Kevin, in fourth grade. He was quiet and a little gawky and I like to imagine he became the kind of guy I would become friends with over and over, hanging out with immediate ease. Once, Kevin mentioned where he lived and I knew the house exactly, a true midwestern split-level at a perpendicular intersection that was much busier than the one where my house was. I saw it all the time because we had to drive past it to get to

Meijer or Saigon Market. He must have heard cars rushing through his dreams. I retain a memory of Kevin telling me, at the end of the school year, that he was moving. But I can't remember where, or why, or if this even happened or if I just wanted it to have happened. I see his face: angular; light blue eyes; a tiny mole on one cheek. By the start of fifth grade, he was gone. I have no idea what happened to him and probably never will, because his common last name renders him unsearchable. Every time I'm in that city and drive past his house (why is it always astonishing when houses are still *there*), I wonder who he is now.

My parents' cottage-looking house in Michigan is almost unrecognizable from the place I knew in my teenage years, at least on the inside. Over the years my dad has replaced every floor, knocked down walls to allow more light. Less and less of that house can remind me of what it was like to finish growing up there, and this is a relief.

My dad, too, is not the person he was when I was growing up. No one is or could be. He and my stepmom are decades past arguing. So why was it hard to imagine this future—the big windows; wanting the company of my family—when I was a kid? Why did I always feel stuck in time? Why did

I think growing up was an escape instead of the return it really is?

In the kitchen, the place where my sister and I have always ended up chatting, she asked about my visit with our mother, and what we talked about, and if I had learned anything new.

I told her that I wasn't exactly sure what she remembered anymore. That she repeated the same things a lot. I don't think she's lonely, I said. She just looks that way.

I guess I should go visit, Anh said.

I said yes, and wasn't her child curious?

A little bit, Anh said. I don't know. I guess we'll try sometime this fall.

We were leaning against the kitchen counter, eating from a bag of tortilla chips. How many times had we done this in our lives? Every time I went back to that house I would think, maybe this will be the last time, maybe they really will sell it, or at least sell the land that it's on, and move, even if I can't imagine to where.

I suggested to Anh that we go down to the basement and see if there were any old boxes or books or things that we might want to keep.

Anh said, Do you know how many spiders live down there? Even Mom and Dad don't go into the basement.

It was true that I hadn't stepped foot down there in more than ten years, and that a long while back my dad and stepmom had thrown out a bunch of boxes ruined by mold and mildew. I didn't know what could possibly be there, that I hadn't been doing just fine without. Still, I remembered that black-and-white photograph of my mother, how I had found it when I was in college. It would be a projection to say that any object was waiting, but it was hard not to think that all the same. But could I even say where that photo was now, or what box I had placed it in for some idea about preservation?

———

My family had started meeting up on Zoom during the early months of the pandemic, as people were doing then. It's been going on ever since, nearly every Sunday. Sometimes just a few people, sometimes everyone—my parents, siblings, cousins, an aunt and uncle, me. We are in various time zones, in various kitchens and living rooms, cooking or eating or hanging out. Sometimes the talk is about work, or plans, or what everyone is doing on a given holiday. Sometimes my uncle reminisces about Vietnam. I've never seen or talked to my family as much as I have during this pandemic.

I think about *The Visitors*, all those musicians on their separate screens in a performance from 2012, long before everyone would know what a novel coronavirus was. In the museums, first in San Francisco and then in Boston, I thought the musicians kept singing, *Once again, I fall in two / My family waits.* Over and over they sing it, playing instruments from a bedroom, in a bathtub, in a drawing room with a grand piano. The words and melody would surface in my mind afterward and I would hum along. Only recently did I think to look up the actual lyrics and found that they had nothing to do with family. *Once again*, they sing, *I fall into my feminine ways.*

I've always been one to mishear lines. Mondegreens, I've learned these are called. Mine are usually preposterous. It's not *lay me down in Ypsilanti*; it's *lay me down in sheets of linen.* But every once in a while, like in those museums, like now, I prefer the mishearing. I can't undo it. *Once again, I fall in two / My family waits* is what I hear; it's what makes sense to me. I live in the uncertainty of such waiting. Is it an impatient kind, a foot tapping on the floor? Or is it safety-net waiting, knowing others are there if it turns out you really do need them? Maybe you don't know until they tell you.

My family, the one I grew up with, loves karaoke, and my brother has played the drums his whole life. But I wouldn't call us musical. We've never been a band. We are more used to being in different rooms of a house that looks to be in the process of serious disrepair. But eventually, we leave our own spaces and converge. Because the habit is strong, and the reward gets better every year. The habit makes the tension of the unsaid bearable, even preferable. Just as sometimes singing is better than talking. Dancing better than sitting. Walking down a forged path, across a meadow, toward water, is better done together.

I thought I was going to Michigan to ask my dad and stepmom about my mother. What they knew and never told me and my sister. What they felt or decided when they were younger, and what they thought of it all now that they were in their seventies. I thought it would be possible to get answers and perspectives about the past, even if I wasn't sure if I would recognize them as such.

But I ended up not asking any of those questions. I didn't revisit, or go searching. I just turned the pages of the old photo albums again, and paid respects to my grandmother's ashes, and paused at the window next to the front door where I had stood so many times as a teenager, trying to see beyond the driveway and the tips of the pine trees in the distance.

And then I went back to hang out with my son and my family, all of us outside in the forgiving late-summer weather of lake-effect Michigan. Later, after food and drink, we would karaoke with some distance between us, each with our own microphone covers. My dad would take my stepmom into his arms and it would be impossible not to watch him glide them across the floor. They would dance right over the buried swimming pool where my siblings and I once floated.

All my life I have felt like an imposter daughter, an imposter Vietnamese, an imposter American, and often an imposter mother, failing and disappointing, an unreliable narrator. When does a refugee stop being a refugee? The answer is in the question itself, forever unanswerable. Whatever my dad and stepmom might tell me, whatever my mother tells me—their stories, their versions, their sides—why do I think I need, or deserve, an actual answer? Why do I think one is even possible?

Outside my parents' cottage house, the raggedy willow trees look dead tired of guarding the pond that's covered in greenish scum—is it algae, is it moss, is it watermeal? Nothing could possibly be reflected there. A small, overturned boat lies down beside it. The long driveway is rutted with potholes now, like the earth beneath it is getting assertive in its reclaiming. Every summer, storms take down more of the trees in the thinning woods, scattering branches that stay scattered across the yard. More feral cats have come to my parents' door, and my parents feed and name them.

In a postapocalyptic story, a group of people would be wandering the overgrown, once-highway-busy road when someone notices a hidden path. Some pavement under the tall grass and weeds. They are curious enough to follow it down, nearly a quarter of a mile, past a small hollow that used to be a pond, to the astonishing sight of a gray A-frame house crumbling into the hill it was built on. The people wonder if the house might be stable enough to enter, to see what might be found there. They wonder, Who lived here? Did they leave on their own, or were they made to?

———

When I am back in the landscape of my childhood, I know it is nothing special. It is as flat and subdivided and big-box as people who've never been here think it is. It is so, so American. Near downtown, some of the brick Victorians have been restored into some rich person's fantasy of what came before, walkable to a gentrified street of little restaurants, shops that sell expensive jam and oven mitts printed with the map of Michigan. That's not my world. If you wanted to understand where I lived and grew up, I would tell you to start at the western edge of 28th Street in Grand Rapids, Michigan, and drive the entirety of it, heading due east, about thirteen miles and countless stoplights and billboards, to where it ends at Cascade Road. You'd see strip malls, empty lots, and shut-down buildings, thrift stores and fast food, a purple-painted adult store called The Velvet Touch, used-car lots and new-car lots, budget motels and newer Ramadas, corporate restaurants and grocery stores, churches and ministries and banks, the newer, bigger Saigon Market and the lot where the original store once stood, its yellow and red sign always in my mind, and so many streets leading to schools and parks you'll never see, the site of a cinder-block club called Electric Avenue, where my sisters used to go, on toward the wine shops and ramen spots that didn't exist when I was a kid, so many miles of traffic and missing turns and wondering how much longer all of this is going to take, well past on-ramps to freeways that will get you away from all of this.

My mother in Boston does not drive on any street. She has never been to Michigan and will never know how I grew up. Is it accurate or is it cruel to say that my mother missed out on so much? Is that a wrong construction, the idea of missing? If we don't know what we missed, did we miss anything at all? Maybe we were simply elsewhere, in a reality that someone else was missing out on, too. Why would she have missed any more than I would have missed?

Here is a thing that I have never said or admitted because it sounds fucked up: every year my children get older feels like such a relief, not just because every year feels like a gain in their health and growth, but also because it feels like every extra year means they will be okay because they will be old enough, and getting older enough, to bear it if something terrible happens. One of the reasons early childhood, and thus early motherhood, is so terrifying is that we are always thinking about danger, worrying about safety and loss. What is worse, the fear of losing your children or the fear of your children losing you? And if your children lost you, would you live enough in their minds? What if they forget, and thus lose you?

I see the direct line from my own childhood, my refugee identity, my own relationship with my mother in Boston, to these anxieties. I see it whenever I sigh with relief at each year that we are allowed to accumulate. I am so mad at time and so grateful for it. Whatever happens, I think now, my children will know me. They will never have to question their origin stories. They will have memories of holidays and national parks, and all those train rides and subway rides and all those walks around cities where we were guests and wanderers. They will have so many pictures as proof. They will remember, too, the everyday. The arguments and tantrums and thrown-together dinners and rushing to school and, yes, all of my failures as a mother.

I wrote down what my mother told me when I saw her in Boston, the sixth visit so far in our lifetimes. She talked about my dad and the relationship they'd had in Saigon. She talked about all the years she had waited to see me and my sister. She talked about how strange life was, sometimes, but that's how it went.

I wrote down what she said, the small details she was finally giving to me. And then deleted them.

I wrote down what she said, the small details, and saved them in a different file, to keep.

I find that I am a writer, writing nonfiction, trying to keep some things for myself. Trying to figure out what is mine, what is time, what is mine to say, what are we doing with words when they begin with someone else?

I am sitting in my house in Wisconsin, at a desk set against an eastern-facing second-floor window, where I have watched leaves fall enough to reveal that yellow door of the gray-shingled shed in someone else's backyard. I see that yellow now, writing this, revising this, and I think about how, in late spring, it will disappear into the greenery of the trees. Sometimes I think this is exactly what my childhood self hoped my future self would get to have: to be at a desk, typing while the daylight closes down in front of her. Why are you reading in the dark? my sisters, my stepmom, my grandmother, would ask me, and I wouldn't know that I was until someone said it. Why are you reading into the dark? I sometimes misheard, in two different ways: as direction, as interpretation. I guess I learned how to do both: to read, into the dark; to read into the dark.

That's me, now, writing in and into the darkness. It's the only way I have left to be who I thought I was, or would be, or could be, before I was anything to anybody. Before anyone could call me a word like *mother*. Before I could understand the concept of *refugee*. My children, when we're at home, still call me Mama. It's startling to think about how they will remember this—how they will remember me. Us. The shards of storytelling are not always sharp. I do not, even now, know who I am writing this for. Maybe for them. Maybe for those of us who long to time-travel, who think we can reconcile the past with words. Maybe for my own mother, who for me has often been more idea than actuality, someone who may never read this and will never need to. When I say mother I am saying loss, I am saying the thing that fights against loss. I am asking you to wait, asking what you will remember from here on out.

ACKNOWLEDGMENTS

This book has been years in the making, and I am deeply grateful to so many people, especially my agent, Nicole Aragi, and my editor, Sally Howe, for guiding the way. Thank you to Kelsey Day, Duvall Osteen, Mark LaFlaur, Lauren Dooley, Brianna Yamashita, Lisa Nicholas, Abigail Novak, Martha Schwartz, Elisa Rivlin, Jonathan Bush, and everyone at Aragi, Inc., and Scribner.

Thank you to all the writers, friends, and editors who have helped me rethink my work and encouraged me to keep going (even if you didn't know it at the time!), including Natalie Bakopoulos, Amy Quan Barry, Hilary Cadigan, Kirstin Chen, Jill Christman, Richard Damstra, Camille Dungy, Peter Ho Davies, Deanna Fei, Lori Fradkin,

ACKNOWLEDGMENTS

V. V. Ganeshananthan, Natalie Eve Garrett, Vanessa Hua, Yuka Igarashi, Amaud Johnson, Lacy M. Johnson, R. O. Kwon, Allisen Lichtenstein, Toni Mirosevich, Dantiel W. Moniz, Aimee Nezhukumatathil, Mehdi Tavana Okasi, Isabelle Thuy Pelaud, Aimee Phan, Joanna Rakoff, Jenna Ryan, Cherene Sherrard, Porter Shreve, Laura Tisdel, Vu Tran, Azareen Van der Vliet Oloomi, Liz Van Hoose, and all of my fantastic colleagues in English and Creative Writing at the University of Wisconsin–Madison.

Most of all, thank you to my family and to my children.

I am grateful to have received support and time to write this book from the Vilas Trust, the Department of English, the College of Arts and Sciences, and the Division of the Arts at the University of Wisconsin–Madison; and from the Corporation of Yaddo.

Parts of this book were previously published, in different form and sometimes with different titles, in the following publications: sections of "Apparent," edited by Emily Nemens and Hasan Altaf for *The Paris Review*, later selected for *Best American Essays 2021*, edited by Robert Atwan and Kathryn Schulz; sections of "The Story of My Name," edited by Michael Agger for *The New Yorker*; sections of "Twenty-Four Hours," edited by Jonny Diamond for *Literary Hub*; sections of "The Photograph," *Requiem for a Paper Bag: Celebrities and Civilians Tell Stories of the Best Lost, Tossed, and Found*

ACKNOWLEDGMENTS

Items from Around the World, edited by Davy Rothbart. With gratitude to all.

This book includes quotes or references from: Yến Lê Espiritu, "Toward a Critical Refugee Study: The Vietnamese Refugee Subject in US Scholarship," *Journal of Vietnamese Studies* 1, nos. 1–2, February/August 2006; Trinh T. Minh-ha, *When the Moon Waxes Red: Representation, Gender and Cultural Politics*, Routledge, 1991; Vinh Nguyen, "Refugee-tude," *Social Text* 37, no. 2, June 2019; Rita Kohli and Daniel G. Solórzano, "Teachers, please learn our names!: racial microaggressions and the K-12 classroom," *Race Ethnicity and Education*, 2012.

ABOUT THE AUTHOR

Beth Nguyen, who has also written under the name Bich Minh Nguyen, is the author of three previous books: the memoir *Stealing Buddha's Dinner* and the novels *Short Girls* and *Pioneer Girl*. She has received an American Book Award and a PEN/Jerard Fund Award, and her work has appeared in numerous anthologies and publications, including *The New Yorker*, *The Paris Review*, *The New York Times*, and *The Best American Essays*. Nguyen teaches creative writing at the University of Wisconsin–Madison.

OWNER OF A LONELY HEART

Beth Nguyen

This reading group guide for OWNER OF A LONELY HEART includes an introduction, discussion questions, and ideas for enhancing your book club. The suggested questions are intended to help your reading group find new and interesting angles and topics for your discussion. We hope that these ideas will enrich your conversation and increase your enjoyment of the book.

INTRODUCTION

Owner of a Lonely Heart is a powerful, lyrical memoir of a mother-daughter relationship fragmented by war and resettlement, from the award-winning author of *Stealing Buddha's Dinner*.

When Beth Nguyen was eight months old, she and her family, excluding her mother, fled Saigon for America. Beth did not meet her mother, who stayed—or was left behind—until Beth was nineteen. Since meeting her mother again (or, really, for the first time) as an adult, Beth and her mother have spent less than twenty-four hours together.

Owner of a Lonely Heart is a memoir that examines identity through parenthood, war, absence, and the condition of being a refugee. It is the story of Beth's relationship with her mother and her relationship with herself. Fragmented and framed by the fleeting interactions between mother and daughter, Beth tells a coming-of-age story that spans her own midwestern childhood, her first meeting with her mother, and becoming a parent herself. Sharp and heartrending, *Owner of a Lonely Heart* is a lyrical story that explores loss and discovery, disconnection and connection, and loneliness and belonging.

TOPICS & QUESTIONS FOR DISCUSSION

1. Beth talks about existing in a liminal, or in-between, space: she is a former refugee who is in between mothers and losses. In what other ways can you see liminality in Beth's life and experiences? How does this "in-betweenness" shape her relationship to other people, and to herself?

2. Beth talks about being astonished by a photograph of her father's motorcycle—it has traveled countless miles and is one of the only family heirlooms they have: it is proof of their history (9). How has Beth's father and his history—physical objects and stories passed down orally—shaped Beth's relationship to herself and her culture?

3. A journal editor once told Beth not to use the word *trauma*, as it "had become meaningless" (134), and the word appears only a few times in the book. Do you think the supposed ubiquity of the word *trauma* in cultural discourse flattens its impact? Consider and discuss the concept of *generational trauma*. How do you think Beth relates to the idea?

4. Mothers are often expected to be heavily involved in their children's lives; they are seen as the force holding families together, and their roles are often scrutinized. At the same time, "mothers aren't supposed to take up so much space" (38). How does gender function in this memoir? How would Beth's story be different if her father was the parent from whom she was estranged?

5. Beth and her mother show affection differently: her mother is "not an emotional person" (37), while Beth, on the other hand, seems to feel deeply and appears ever concerned with her children's feelings and experiences. Beth's mother shows affection by making sure the children have eaten and by eagerly offering them mango juice (32). How do you think Beth's and her mother's different upbringings have influenced their styles of parenting and showing affection?

6. How did your understanding of forgiveness shift throughout the story, especially as you read about *why* Beth's mother was absent?

7. What is Beth referencing with the title *Owner of a Lonely Heart*? Do you think being an "owner of a lonely heart" is a permanent state?

8. Consider the relationship between Beth and her siblings, in both childhood and adulthood. How has their upbringing shaped their bond?

9. In chapter 8, "White Mothers," Beth refers to her (white) high school boyfriend Evan, and his mother, Celia. Beth describes her relationship with Celia, in tender detail, as a "respite from daily life" (168). How did Beth's relationship with Celia influence her understanding of or experience with race?

10. The author does not provide an answer to many seemingly unanswerable questions, such as: *When does a refugee stop being a refugee?* (229), and *What is worse, the fear of losing your children or the fear of your children losing you?* (232). Discuss these questions and possible answers.

ENHANCE YOUR BOOK CLUB

1. Read Beth's previous memoir, *Stealing Buddha's Dinner*, and her novels, *Short Girls* and *Pioneer Girl*.

2. Think about your own family history and the ways in which families are made—by birth or by circumstances over which you have no control. Explore the ways in which the lives of your family, before or after your own birth, have affected your upbringing and current relationships.

3. Beth's story is just one of many that are related to the Vietnam War and its impacts. Research other stories—fiction and nonfiction, such as the documentary *Daughter from Danang* and Viet Thanh Nguyen's novel *The Sympathizer*.